The Good City

Cities, Allan B. Jacobs contends, ought to be magnificent, beautiful places to live. They should be places where people can be fulfilled, where they can be what they can be, where there is freedom, love, ideas, excitement, quiet, and joy. Cities ought to be the ultimate manifestation of society's collective achievements.

Jacobs is one of the world's best-known planners and urban design practitioners, with a long and distinguished international career. Drawing on his professional experience of almost 60 years, he guides the reader through the lessons he's learned as a planner and lover of cities.

Starting from a childhood in Cleveland, where he learned to explore and enjoy the city, Jacobs takes us through the development of his fascination with the urban environment. Throughout his career, he has worked in India, Brazil, Italy, Japan, and China as well as many of the U.S.'s greatest cities, most notably as San Francisco's planning director in the tumultuous 1960s and 1970s. Essays, fiction, and case studies from these locations convey to the reader a wealth of knowledge which can be gained only through passionate experience.

Featuring a wonderfully engaging, humorous tone and Jacobs' own drawings, *The Good City* transfers lessons on city design, building and urban change to all those willing to help cities become the magnificent, beautiful places they should be—and encourages all inhabitants to learn to appreciate and explore their own cities.

Allan B. Jacobs has almost 60 years of active city planning and urban design practice, research, and teaching experience in major American and world cities. He served as San Francisco's planning director during the 1960s and 1970s, a period of both confrontation and historic urban design achievement. Prior to that Jacobs worked in Cleveland, Pittsburgh during its "renaissance" years, and Calcutta, India, before teaching at the University of Pennsylvania. He has consulted and worked in Curitiba, Brazil, Rome, Japan, Shanghai, Abu Dhabi, Vancouver, and many U.S. cities. Presently, he is Professor Emeritus at the Department of City and Regional Planning, University of California, Berkeley, and Professor in the Graduate School there.

Looking toward St. Peter's

The Good City

Reflections and Imaginations

Allan B. Jacobs

Routledge
Taylor & Francis Group

LONDON AND NEW YORK

First published 2011
by Routledge
2 Park Square, Milton Park, Abingdon, Oxon, OX14 4RN

Simultaneously published in the USA and Canada
by Routledge
270 Madison Avenue, New York, NY 10016

*Routledge is an imprint of the Taylor & Francis Group, an informa
business*

Typeset in Univers by
Keystroke, Station Road, Codsall, Wolverhampton
Printed by
Edwards Brothers, Inc.

British Library Cataloguing in Publication Data
A catalogue record for this book is available from the British Library

Library of Congress Cataloging-in-Publication Data
Jacobs, Allan B.
    The good city : reflections and imaginations / Allan B. Jacobs.
        p. cm.
    Includes bibliographical references and index.
    1. City planning. 2. City and town life. I. Title.
    HT166.J2618 2011
    307.1'216—dc22   2010023232

ISBN13: 978–0–415–59350–2 (hbk)
ISBN13: 978–0–415–59353–3 (pbk)
ISBN13: 978–0–203–83596–8 (ebk)

To Elizabeth
And to
Johan, Anders, Katharine, Bjorn,
Rachel, Danny, and Zachary

Contents

Acknowledgments

For almost 20 years I have had the good fortune to recall (and probably exaggerate) early city experiences and to share ideas about them with my partner in everything, Elizabeth Macdonald. I have shown and read my writings to her and listened to advice and critiques from her. What enlarging opportunities I have had, many while we were working on professional projects together. What wonderful luck! She has encouraged and helped me all along the way.

For over 20 years, until 2007, Kaye Bock, at the University of California, Berkeley, turned my longhand into printed pages, editing many of the first drafts of the pieces that appear here. Then, without preparation, she died. She is very much remembered and the thank-yous don't stop.

Super-editor for all my previous books, Amy Jacobs, read and commented on the introduction for this work, and her words were a good enough OK to proceed. Janet and Matthew, who lived the Calcutta experience, with Amy, read and implied my continuance with the "Why India?" piece. Marcia McNally and Randy Hester did careful reviews with suggestions on the "Why India?" essay, and Nezar AlSayyed and Ananya Roy reviewed the piece as well. Jaime Lerner, dear friend and colleague for many years, along with Fani, his wife, was kind enough to review the Curitiba essay, correct some early errors, and remind me of a project or two that I had forgotten.

Over the years, I have experienced and enjoyed, many times, the facilities, comforts, and friendships offered at the American Academy in Rome. "Gianicolo Busts" was written there, "The Etcher of Caprano" was inspired there, development of my drawing and watercolor hand, such as it is, came from time in the studio there and from countless days walking the streets of Rome. At the Academy, Pina Pasquantonio's many welcomings and care are emblematic of all the others who have been so helpful over the years. Lorenzo Bruno, master etcher, printer, and painter, certainly had a lot to do with the art and the etching and the knowledge of the many small communities that we visited, as well as of L'Aquila. Riccardo Wallach and Paolo Ceccarelli have hosted and advised me so often.

If positive accomplishments were possible during my tenure as San Francisco's planning director, they could not have happened without some wonderful and very skilled staff professionals. Some are mentioned by name in the text that follows. Peter Svirsky stands out as the consummate esteemed professional. Bruce Anderson continues to remind me of important incidents that I forget. I thank so many others, mentioned or not. Their recollections and assessments of what we did and either the lasting or non-existent value of our undertakings may be different than mine, and that's fine.

Richard Legates was more than helpful in directing me to the Routledge people and I am most grateful. Louise Fox has herded me through the initial phases of publication and I thank her no end.

Finally, the early start of what is now my view of what makes a good city was with Donald Appleyard, when we wrote *Toward a New Urban Design Manifesto*. Donald is gone, but not really.

Part I

Experiencing Cities

An Introduction

This is a book born of growing up in what was once a real city, Cleveland, in the 1930s and early 1940s, and of being excited by visiting and learning how to get around in cities, particularly New York City. It was nurtured by the experiences of working in and for cities as a professional city planner–urban designer for many years, and of continued travel in them and walking, walking, walking their streets, all the time looking at what was to be seen, their physicality and the people who inhabit them, of always asking why things are the way they are, and of drawing and recording them, with some relentlessness.

Yes, Cleveland remained a real city in the 1930s and through the 1940s. It had a downtown with the very tall Terminal Tower as a focal point to mark its center and the big city New York Central railroad station beneath it, a busy public square where streetcars from the east and west sides converged and turned around, four or five department stores, and a core concentration of first-run movie palaces up Euclid Avenue. There were universities, a celebrated symphony hall and art museum, and it had all the heavy and light industry that any city could want. As World War II broke out it was said that if an enemy wanted to put the U.S. war effort out of commission it would bomb Cleveland; so many products key to industrial production, like heavy machine tools and ball bearings, were made there. And the population, ethnically diverse, with many Eastern Europeans, was grow- ing; blue and white collar together. The population of the city would reach almost one million by 1960. Cleveland stretched along Lake Erie, with the Cuyahoga River (yes, the polluted one that would soon catch fire) dividing it in two, an east and west side. The lake front and what it might offer for recreation was largely ignored in favor of industry, but there was always hope of something better.

A young boy growing up in that environment could and did learn early about using the streetcars and buses, most memorably the former, to get around and explore the city. Depending on where you lived, one or two streetcars or a streetcar and a bus got you downtown. There were choices of streetcars with almost the same, but different enough, routes. They came often. An elementary school kid could find his way around the whole city. In Cleveland Heights, the first suburb east of the city, there were three lines to choose from. There were plenty of local places to go on foot or bicycle; you didn't have to go downtown to be on crowded streets or to the movie houses. There were four or five movies at 105th Street and Euclid, to say nothing of the commercial skating rink and the art museum and park just beyond. And there were many small and not-so-small stores from which, if a kid without money could not buy anything, he could at least window-shop and dream. The Cleveland Public Library, downtown, welcomed kids, especially those who needed to work on a paper – one that was overdue – for school. And, on school-skipping days, usually Thursdays, a truant could head downtown, wait for a movie at the RKO Palace to end and then join all the departees, but walk unnoticed, backward, among them, to gain free access to the next show. The west side was something of a mystery to an east-sider, but one knew the main streets, like Lorain Avenue, lined with small stores in two-storey buildings, apartments above, and also with streetcars, streets that seemed to run for ever, even out to the airport. And a food market with many stalls was in the near west side among Eastern European churches with onion-shaped steeples and community halls and nearby bars that advertised live polka music on weekends.

But Clevelanders, especially on the east side, kept moving toward the suburbs, further and further out. That might have been fine as long as new people kept coming to the city, but that didn't happen. The flight outward was helped by street widenings, one-way streets, and, in time, freeways, and by replacing streetcars with buses, to make the streets more favorable to autos. The city seemed hell bent to achieve, as quickly as possible, the vision promised by the General Motors' "World of Tomorrow" exhibit at the New York World Fair of 1939 and 1940. No one seemed to question the wisdom of doing that. Downtown, and even the secondary urban shopping centers, became harder to reach. Voter-approved bond funds for a downtown subway were not issued, not once, but twice, over two six-year periods. The freeway men were in charge, particularly the County Engineer. Decision after decision favored suburban sprawl. The vision was of freeways, in physical shape like the new Pennsylvania Turnpike, running through beautiful rolling countryside, the cars always moving, no one thinking to anticipate congestion. People less well-to-do, mostly black, replaced the fleers for a while.

The "long hot summers" of the mid- and late 1960s, the days of race riots, saw major conflagrations in Cleveland, vast areas set to the torch by angry minority people who had been left behind. And, though Cleveland's population today is less than half of what it was at its height, with no population growth, the outward migration moves onward, consuming a once-beautiful rolling landscape with housing on large lots and new shopping centers that replace not-so-old ones; an environmental nightmare. The hole in the doughnut, the vacant central city, grows larger. Now it is hard to call Cleveland a city.

Of course, a same or similar story could be told for many of the older industrial, so-called rust-belt cities of the East and Midwest. Try Detroit or St. Louis or Kansas City. Of the latter, in 1980 it was appropriate for me to write an essay, "They're Locking the Doors to Downtown," to characterize a new inward-oriented shopping center/hotel complex across from the landmark railroad station, a center that would draw urban activities and people further from the central downtown. By 2005 the number of retail and service stores in the whole of downtown Kansas City could be counted on the fingers of one hand. Vacancy was everywhere and the dominant view, on every downtown street, was of a parking garage.

A kid growing up in Cleveland, then, one who loved to explore its many areas by walking or public transit, captivated without knowing why by all that was seen and experienced, people, buildings, stores, parks and squares, store windows, tree-lined streets, such a kid would soon enough bemoan what was being lost, but would by that time have found other cities that beckoned.

New York City was the first to captivate. A teenager who had grandparents, an uncle, and other family in New York, and was thrilled by the activity, the variety, all the people, the bigness, and the many physical things, moving or still, that capture the eyes and keep them moving, was a lucky youngster indeed. In Cleveland, there was nothing to compare with Joyce Kilmer Park, opposite the Bronx County Court House alongside the Grand Concourse, an urban square to walk to with a grandfather or an uncle, meet people of at least two generations that they kibitzed with, buy a Dixie cup or a pretzel, watch the people. Yankee Stadium was nearby, the Polo Grounds not far off. A corner store sold "Jew beers," chocolate phosphates. One could walk all the way up to Fordham Road to take in a matinée at the Loews Paradise, or hang a right and visit the Bronx Zoo. The Bronx, too, would be torn apart in the late 1960s and 1970s by the Cross-Bronx Expressway, as has been chronicled by many, perhaps most notably by Marshall Berman in *All That Is Solid Melts into Air*.

Earlier, though, a subway ride took a young teenager to mid-town and beyond, emerging, to walk along the streets and avenues – Fifth Avenue not the least – from the library to Central Park, always with a stop at Rockefeller Center; very heady, sophisticated stuff for a young man. Take the subway, walk the streets, walk the streets, even get dressed up to walk the streets and look and look and look, entranced, for no particular purpose or reason. Purpose would come later.

Clearly, I am talking about myself, as a child, teenager, and young adult. Being in and getting to know cities, mostly by looking while walking, was just plain fun. If I were to analyze now the why of my early fascination I might say that it was a combination of inherent impatience – Grandmother always said that I had no "*zits fleisch*," but then she didn't have any either – and the reality that good cities keep my eyes and brain moving. Perhaps, too, there was a piece of Willa Cather's "Paul's Case" in me, an unfocused need for an exciting, sophisticated, cultured, and (shame to say) wealthier life – at least more well-to-do than I was ever likely to be. Cities and their people, in part or in whole, captivated.

Without stopping even to recognize a passion for cities, let alone consciously charting a future that might bring me to studying and working in them, I seem to have pulled and pushed that way. Many futures "just happen."

City planning education, regardless of how one came to it, from architecture or landscape architecture or from one of the social sciences, was in the beginning of a major change in the mid-1950s. The traditional focus on the physical arrangements of urban places, the what should go where, why, how and when to meet the needs of residents and workers, consistent with the nature and imperatives of the land itself, was giving way to an emphasis on land and market economics, on urban societal problems such as adequate housing for the poor and on racial inequities, and very much on something called "urban process" or "planning theory." These might be very important matters, more important than the physical, design nature of urban places, but they were becoming so at the expense of three-dimensional urban form. Unless, of course, one was lucky enough to have classroom contact with Lewis Mumford, who, while writing *The City in History*, taught a course on the history of cities and city planning at the University of Pennsylvania and took students on walks in Philadelphia; looking and more looking and pondering what was there. Lucky, too, the student who found Bill Wheaton at either Harvard or the University of Pennsylvania. Economist though he was, Bill focused much of his teaching on the physical city and on field research. Learning about the physical history and design of cities, always in relation to the social and economic forces at work, which Mumford and Wheaton excelled in teaching, proved critical to my development, at the same time that it spurred a soon-to-be professional to want to see more of old and new urban places. Learning to analyze form, particularly relative scale, was formative as well. John Paul Carlhian, at Harvard, challenged students to build models of urban projects, measure, study, and analyze the works of the design big shots of the period, like Corbusier CIAM designs and Stein's garden city superblocks, so that one knew what they looked like and why they worked – or, more often, did not. But these mentors were already becoming exceptions to where the field in general was going and to where it would race in the coming decades. Observing the city planning field over many years from both inside and outside the academy, and reflecting on how its practitioners have increasingly been educated and how that relates to the current nature of city design, one can hardly refrain from reviewing the connection between education and professional practice, with disconsolate sadness, to be sure.

Most of what follows, though, is from personal experience in doing city design, from studying urban physical environments, from travel, and from imagination. Personal experience is not always highly regarded in academic circles associated with cities, at least not as a basis for conclusions as to what physical qualities might, more than others, make a good city. Nonetheless, it seems impossible, after a long professional life, not to come to some conclusions as to what physical characteristics are at least more likely to be associated with the best urbanism and those less likely to be so. Of course, personal bias – call it prejudice even – is involved. It always is, even in the so-called objective conclusions of scientific studies. One's professional experience *is* research, and needs to be reflected more and disseminated, hopefully with the underlying values clearly evident.

This book is made up of both essays and short stories, mostly the former. Readers will know or think they know which is which. Chronology is less important than groupings of essays and stories that reflect on a subject matter and sources of learning, and which build to a concluding essay on "The Good City": the physical, desirable, buildable characteristics in respectful relationships with their environmental contexts, that are much more likely to produce fine, satisfying, sustainable communities for urban life than are other arrangements. The opening essay, "Why India?", was written last but is located where it is because my Calcutta years, which came after almost a decade of professional work in Cleveland and Pittsburgh, were in many ways freeing years that led to looking at urban life in new, more open ways: they freed me from the parts of my education that I needed to escape. Perhaps more importantly, the essay speaks of professional, personal, and ethical issues associated with working in a culture far different than one's own. There are unavoidable connections with national policies related to Vietnam, Iraq, and Afghanistan.

Many of the short essays and stories that bridge between the longer opening and closing pieces were written between and around drawings, field measurements, and notes in sketchbooks that I carried (and still carry) with me, starting in the mid-1970s. At that time I became intent upon improving my graphic skills, dare I say "art" skills, long ignored, and so, in addition to pages of street-plan and cross-section measurements and drawings of people, streets and plazas, as well as notes about what I was seeing, I began to let my mind expand on the potentials of what was in front of me.

Standing one day upon Rome's Gianicolo, drawing the marble busts, I did actually see a woman with a small dog look up with solemnity at the face of General Avezanna, then cross herself before hurriedly moving on, stopping at a likeness of no other famous personage. The event cried out to be recorded and from there it was no effort to slide into fantasy of who she was, of potential celebrations of all the other nation builders, and on to a proposal for Market Street in San Francisco, leading to the "Gianicolo Busts" story. Drawing the church and religious complex across the ravine from the busy central street of Caprarola, before walking along it and to one of its meat shops and the antici-pated crusty roast pork panini that awaited, I could not help but think about the separation of that beautiful institution and its privileged setting, so near and yet so far from the center of the town, and to reflect on the larger implications of such a location, particularly for U.S. urbanism. So the "Being Apart" piece was written, and a drawing was sketched. Roast pork panini together with deep ruminations about urbanism? It happens that way, at least for me.

Much of my writing is rooted in Italy, particularly Rome, a love affair that started in 1982. On my first day there, ostensibly to write the manuscript that would become my second book, *Looking at Cities*, I came to know that if, as a pedestrian, I simply paid no attention to the auto traffic, but walked purposely, cars would not hit me; I was safe. That's an important finding, for which there are certainly many explanations, even ones that may not be universally appreciated; don't try it in Brazil, for example. Certainties, simple truths about urbanism, are born of such experiences, about traffic and parking and change, and land economics, so there is a small section on them – basic urban truths.

The long affair with Italy has been and continues to be a source of learning and inspiration. Why and how does Rome continue to function, not only as a major tourist center and place of immense historic interest, but as a working city, physically and economically? Why do so many things work that present norms and standards say do not or should not work – and which would not be allowed today – in North American cities? Are there not major lessons or adaptations, as opposed to tearing things down and starting over, to be learned from Rome? Why would we not be allowed to replicate, not copy, a condition that we admire in Rome, or for that matter in Paris or an American city, if we wanted to? Observations and ruminations, stemming from Rome and elsewhere in Italy, Europe, and Asia, were the sources of *Great Streets* and *The Boulevard Book*, written with Elizabeth Macdonald and Yodan Rofé. But they were also the source of my story on tourism, "The Etcher of Caprano," of the essay on Via Costa Masciarelli in now-devastated L'Aquila, and certainly the "Memos on Pudong," about world-class cities and discarded advice about development proposals for Pudong, across the river from Shanghai.

All good cities, certainly not Rome alone, are great people-watching environments. This business of city building and design is driven by needs to enable and satisfy people, after all. Drawing gives great opportunities for watching people: they dart in and out of a field of vision; they congregate in some places and not in others. They are easy to talk with, especially when they see you drawing and if you speak their language. Some very consciously work at taking part in and even making "community." A small group of stories is about city people in their environments.

You never truly know what or who will greet you in a new city. And so it was, toward the end of 1975, that I found myself in a city of which I'd never before heard – Curitiba, Brazil. Jaime and Fani Lerner, and their colleagues, were well embarked on monumental changes – functional, physical, social – to their city. Their inventions would continue for over 25 years, to be celebrated and copied elsewhere. Lucky me to have met the place and its people and to have been invited back time and again, and to be able to tell just a few of their city-making achievements and the positivism that has driven them.

As San Francisco's director of city planning from 1967 to 1975, I was driven to distraction by the very strong civil service system which, to my way of thinking, made it nearly impossible to attract and hire top-notch staff if one played by all of its rules. Could I have been put in jail for some of the things I did to circumvent that system? Probably not. But I could have got into trouble. I swore that I would one day enlighten locals and the world about the workings of the system with a detailed exposé. On leaving the city and faced with the mountains of work and time necessary to tell the dreadful story with objective accuracy, I decided that my mother had not brought me up to do that kind of muckraking. And so I wrote a humor piece instead, my first-ever short story, "The Civil Service Giants," which *Harpers* was good enough to publish, encouraging license to undertake other fiction pieces. That story, now some 25 years old, goes with the "Reflecting on San Francisco" essay.

The latter was perhaps the most difficult piece in the collection. I revisited my first book, *Making City Planning Work*, which chronicled my time as San Francisco's planning director, had some second thoughts on the value of what was accomplished during those years, and ruminated on the directions of the city and city planning. The challenge with such reflections is to avoid being an "old scold" – to see the positives and learn some lessons. Hopefully I have done that, always aware of the pitfalls of being a non-objective participant observer.

My fascination with cities started with moving around them, with spending serious time on their streets, with looking and being captivated by what I saw. It is one thing to walk and observe and talk with people along the way. It is quite another to draw and take down, via notes and sometimes measurements, what you see, in sketchbooks. Drawing, however poorly or well (it always improves with time), forces us to look more closely at what is there. Drawing is a way of learning. At the same time it can be a spur to ideas and fantasies: that is, to essays and to short fiction, if one takes the license to do that. And so, drawings from my notebooks are sprinkled throughout the book, to let the relationship continue.

In over 25 years of teaching, I have concluded that undergraduate students can be lighthearted and appreciate and partake of humor; that students at the Master's degree level are in the process of losing what humor they have had and laugh much less; and that most students at the doctorate level have little or no humor, beaten and intent as they are on emulating their professors, who, with rare exception, have none at all. It may not be the academic approach, but there is joy and humor in cities: rules not followed but with no harm done to others, human adaptations to physical conditions that don't work well, an understanding that one's neighbors' obscene construction will not be the end of the world and is even worth a chuckle. Hopefully, some lightheartedness in what follows is evident.

Elsewhere, some 30 years ago, I wrote of my belief that cities ought to be magnificent, beautiful places to live. They should be places where people can be fulfilled, where they can be what they can be, where there is freedom, love, ideas, excitement, quiet, and joy. Cities ought to be the ultimate manifestation of a society's collective achievements. City planning, to me, is the art of helping cities to become and stay that way. Those values remain and have been the driving force in what follows.

Part II

Learning from Calcutta

Calcutta street scene

Drawing from photo by Steve McCurry, Phaidon Press Ltd.

Why India?

Why India? Why on earth did I ever consider, let alone pick up and move to Calcutta in 1963, and do it with a wife and three young kids? What possessed me – us, really – to do that?

We were living in Pittsburgh in 1962. After seven years with the Pittsburgh Regional Planning Association, a well-heeled nonprofit city planning group funded by Pittsburgh's private power structure, I had become assistant director. Richard King Mellon was its president; I once estimated that his income per minute, based only on his known holdings, was significantly larger than was mine in a year. The infrequent board meetings of the Association were held at the Duquesne Club, a place where at that time I would never be permitted as a member, had I wished to be one. I was never comfortable there: visions of Peter Arno cartoons with old men slumped in overstuffed leather chairs, clipping bond coupons and watching the hoi polloi pass on the street outside. There was never an occasion to speak with Mr. Mellon, which was fine with me. I was earning my professional place in the city. Two years earlier we had bought a house for $18,000 that I had been fixing; a wonderful house on a narrow street made of wood blocks, lined with sycamore trees. My wife, through work with the League of Women Voters and political activism with the Democrats, was becoming known and respected. Older daughter Amy had started school. I walked with her to her first day, a year earlier, when Jane was giving birth to Janet. Son Matthew, then three years old, was with friends that day. In short, we were a young, up-and-coming professional family.

A telephone call, just before we were to go on a two-week summer vacation, was from someone representing the Ford Foundation. He'd got my name from Bill Wheaton, my professor at Harvard and Penn: Bill had suggested that I might be just the person for a team being organized by the Foundation to advise the government of West Bengal on a plan for the metropolitan area of Calcutta. Might I be interested? If I had a mentor in graduate school, Bill Wheaton was it. So I said I'd be up to finding out more, which led, a year later, to Calcutta.

I knew next to nothing about India and less about Calcutta: newsreels of Mahatma Gandhi on hunger strikes; *The Four Feathers*, an Alexander Korda film; Indian independence from Britain; Indian restaurants in London; a meaningless (to me) phrase – "the black hole of Calcutta." That was about it; no real knowledge, no particular interest or disinterest, few Indian acquaintances beyond Rabindra Gupta, who had come to work in our offices, fresh from Harvard. Then why even consider the prospect and why, ultimately, make the move?

An idea coming from Bill Wheaton was taken seriously. He seemed to be keeping tabs on me, helping to chart my career, had got me a good summer job in Cleveland and had pointed me to my current boss, Pat Cusick, in Pittsburgh. He thought this might interest me, that working for the Ford Foundation was an opportunity that could open up future possibilities, wide-ranging ones. But he said as well that if I didn't want this job, there would be others. So I can't say that he was pushing me; and certainly I was old enough to make up my own mind, and my mind had never thought of Calcutta (which I had to find on a map). Maybe it was time to move. We'd been in Pittsburgh for almost seven years. Most young city planners those days moved after two or three years in their first jobs. In the previous year I had considered but turned down jobs in Washington and upstate New York, so maybe, though happy in Pittsburgh, I was looking for a chance for advancement, whatever that might mean, or simply for change. Money? For sure we were made aware of the tax advantages of being out of the country for an extended period, meaning that my income would go up by over half. But the jobs I had turned down were also well-paying ones. Adventure? Maybe, but why India?

Some people who had been in Calcutta tried to talk us out of going, noting mostly the poverty, the dirt, the lack of sanitation, the potential for catching exotic diseases, the difficulties of living in such a culturally different place. But the slides and pictures they sent to make their points didn't correspond to their words. Later I would learn that if you really want to show Calcutta, it's better to do it in black and white than in color. The warnings, if one can call them that, were generally without specifics, nothing to fix on. In the year-long discussions and negotiations with the Ford people about my position and roles, and with the team leaders that were being assembled, Jane and I spent considerable time discussing whether to take the plunge. I don't recall either of us asking clearly, or pointedly, "Why are we thinking about this?" or anyone else asking either. In the end, I can't explain why I or we did it. I had no clear purpose, no real goal, and no end to be achieved. For sure, it was a place that needed help, or so I was led to believe, and I'm a sucker for helping: a desire to do good in a place and for people who need assistance. Jane may have had more definable reasons associated with Eastern spirituality, but she never said so. Perhaps she was looking for change. Her graduate education, after all, had been in international relations. I cannot explain why I or we did it. This was not the first time that I made a large life-changing decision without quite knowing why. But it was probably the biggest. Without knowing it, maybe I was bored: looking for excitement. Maybe it was that I was coming on 35 years old and the years alone were what prompted me, us. But what is so special about being 35? There was no big, clear reason for going to Calcutta, India! Daughter Amy says that it was because I wanted to see and get to know the world, that I had had a taste of wider than Midwest and Eastern U.S. experience during a Fulbright fellowship year in England, after graduate school, in the mid-1950s, and that I wanted, needed, to satisfy my curiosity and a need to learn. Maybe. But I don't remember them as conscious reasons at the time.

The move to Calcutta was by way of Cleveland (family), San Francisco, Honolulu, Tokyo, and Hong Kong. Four years later, Matthew, by then eight years old, would resist our moving to San Francisco because he identified it with India and he wanted no more of that kind of living. Jane was more than a little uncomfortable in sweltering, humid August in Tokyo and Hong Kong, but not because of the climate. The short stay in Tokyo coincided with an anniversary of the atomic bombing of Hiroshima and she felt very self-conscious about that: the Japanese must hate us; were we personally accountable? In Hong Kong a fear of the Orient emerged for her. Where was the taxi taking us? A dread of getting into a small dhow that would deliver us to one of the floating restaurants, not far off-shore. Tastes of initial uneasiness to come in Calcutta, starting with an incredible drive in evening half-light from Dum Dum Airport through smoke from evening fires, crowds, cows, people forms, shadows, smells and noises, to an empty (save for the beds) New Alipore villa and bowing servants. The crates bringing our thought-to-be-needed personal household items from Pittsburgh would eventually arrive and sit unopened in the driveway for what seemed like weeks, presumably guarded by the watchman, who never failed to salute as my car came through the gate, but who may or may not have been concerned with the safety of the crates. There they would sit until Jane could bring herself to accept that we would likely be staying a while, and couldn't rush back to safer shores. Nonsense: of course we could have gone back.

The descent toward Dum Dum, Calcutta, on August 20, 1963, in the late afternoon. The waters below have changed from blue to muddy brown; the land is olive, deep olive greens and browns. Colors merge, forms blend to create a vast, flat, fluctuating expanse of muddy land and thick waters. Light monsoon rain sprinkles the plane's small windows; groves of palm trees merge below and help distinguish water from land.

More trees, dark green, in clusters or groves. The rain has stopped. Bleached red and orange-tiled roofs of houses and huts emerge, some orderly yards and fields, a few roads running past them. Some flat tar roofs behind large parapets suggest substantial buildings half hidden in the dark green. The asphalt runway: "You are not permitted to take photographs in the airport. The temperature outside is 92 degrees. The relative humidity is 99 percent. Thank you for traveling on British Overseas Airline Company."

The drive to the city in the evening half-light. The Dum Dum Arsenal and Clive's House pass in rapid succession. "Clive of India," builder of the British Empire. I had thought the dum dum bullet a Chicago gang invention. Now the name registers; this is where it was invented and first produced. Clive's House: once a large mansion, now crumbling and yellowed in the dusk, its walls half fallen away behind a raggle-taggle wilderness of unkempt green. Small groups of people on its verandah, huddled over smoky fires – refugees from East Bengal, our driver tells us. Traffic increases, traffic of all kinds – people, lorries, cars, cycles, rickshaws, carts, bullocks, cows, goats, and dogs. The narrow road serves them all. Our car stops, starts, weaves in and out. Its horn bleats continually. No one pays attention. People are beginning to cook their evening meals. Black smoke hangs heavy from a thousand small dung fires. There is a potpourri of strange and unpleasant smells. We pass small lumber mills, skirting ditches along the road that are full of dark and dubious water. As we draw nearer center city, the number of people flowing into and along the roads increases; within an inch of our car windows children are playing, men are squatting and talking, people are pounding on metal, cooking, or stopping to shop at the tiny open stalls that line the road. These are mostly one-storey, bamboo, wood, and corrugated metal shacks, open to the street, like three-walled huts; largely unlit, occasionally with a fire or a single bare bulb inside; each one a store or a tiny industry where the customer stands at the threshold to shop or order. Low-hanging smoke seems to infest everything with dinginess; people, buildings, animals, and the inevitable cows. Not the picture-book cows with which a Westerner is familiar. Here the cows are dirty-gray and small; full-grown, but small. They have strange, bony structures at the tail and odd hollows beneath their ribs; stringy teats hanging slack under their bellies. A sad, dwarfed race, they seem oblivious to the crowd around them, to our horn, to the car as it inches past.

More of the approaching city: streetlights, neon lights, traffic lights at an intersection. A policeman in white shorts and black belt is calmly sorting out and directing lorries, cars, hand-drawn carts, buses, and streetcars in what seems to be a first-class traffic jam. Pedestrians and cows are beneath his notice. Metallic music comes from some ancient radio, joining a furor of auto horns. We clear the intersection and are grateful for a new sense of openness and a small breeze against the wetness of our clothes and skin. Now travel is fast and ordered down a wide main street, Chittaranjan Avenue. Here there are curbs and sidewalks, and tall substantial buildings; most seem cracked and worn, but nothing is very distinguishable under the poor streetlighting. More lights and openness on a street recognized from travel books and guides, Chowringhee: the Grand Hotel, white and rambling with a red neon sign; the Maidan, now just a broad, open field in the darkness; the Victoria Memorial, a solid, massive white marble structure, rising out of the dark; the racecourse.

We enter Alipore Road and pass the zoo and National Library in rapid succession. In the darkness one can see trees and walls, only an occasional glimpse of large dark houses beyond them.

Suddenly we are "home." Five servants appear from no place. Five pre-selected servants with strange names and duties in a strange, large, empty six-room house with sixteen-foot ceilings, stone floors, and echoes. A flurry of confused, undirected activity – but we are too tired to do anything but go to bed. I go to the toilet. As I stand there I see a small – very small – lizard on the wall. In the morning, on the front page of *The Statesman*, there is an article about a favorite elephant at the zoo, one that had given rides to thousands of children. It had suddenly gone berserk the night before, had broken out of its cage, killed its mahout keeper, and started for the tiger cages. Zookeepers had shot and killed it.

Notes from early days:

- An ochre stucco covers most buildings, dark and streaked with black mold, cracked and revealing a soft and equally cracked red brick. The same ochre stucco, hand-worn and dirty, in heavy, sugary, wedding-cake balconies and screens, imitations of lace-like stone and wood-carved counterparts by earlier and better craftsmen rising the full façade of old buildings and, together with faded green shutters and sleepy palms or feathery gol mohurs, reminiscent of decaying parts of the American South. Occasional structures, sometimes new, more often newly painted, in white or fresh ochre that sparkles in the sun, question, by their existence, whether Calcutta is so run down or simply in need of a coat of paint.
- Beggars of every shape, size, sex, age, and physical condition, persistently following and following their targets with the constant "Baksheesh, I am hungry, no mama, no papa, give me money, baksheesh, no khana." Men, squatting, backs to the street, relieving themselves when and where they can; men bathing at the public water taps or tube wells along the streets, reminders, like the constantly attended, well-groomed hair, of a need and desire for cleanliness, satisfied in brown, unfiltered Hooghly River water.
- One-storey clay huts with tile or corrugated-metal roofs, 120 square feet to the family, cramped together and separated by three-foot-wide alleys, in bustees (supposedly the worst of the slums) with open sewers and no plumbing.
- Daily cholera statistics; the Calcutta Corporation, debating on whether or not to continue the one-year experiment of chlorinating the unfiltered water supply, an experiment started the year before during an increase in cholera cases.
- Women, especially old and bent women, forever sweeping dirt and dust away from earthen thresholds.
- Dark and poorly maintained interiors of most buildings, ochre again with deep-red betel-juice stain in the corners.

Street scene, Calcutta – Ward 20

- Walled streets in Old Calcutta, with occasional openings behind which may be magnificent lawns and homes sealed off from the public ways and the usually ill-maintained public realm, suggesting a more subtle urban aesthetic than that found in Western cities and at the same time a distaste for the city and urban life.

- Expensive estates and flats, smart shops, exorbitant "key money" for any new lease; a construction boom, barely noticeable amid the inertia of ill-maintained, old buildings and pot-holed streets, in new homes and apartments for the "middle" classes along the streets. They are grabbed up the minute they come on the market. Expensive, air-conditioned restaurants, dimly lit with an international décor, Western or Indian food, a small band with an attractive singer (almost always Anglo-Indian) at night, an off-key violin playing music of the 1930s at lunch, plenty of saris but not a dhoti in sight, only ties and jackets.

- Sophisticated parties with plenty of food and drink where the first comment always seems to be "Planning Calcutta, eh? Do you think there's a hope?" or, "What are you going to do about this city? The Corporation is so corrupt," or something about democracy being a Western concept and the need for a strong man, benevolent of course. "I'm just a common citizen, it would be hopeless for me to get involved in local politics. What can the ordinary citizen do? It's impossible." From a businessman or intellectual or almost anyone: "The Marwaris control everything"; "We were inundated by refugees at Partition and have never been able to recover"; "Calcutta is full of immigrants from Bihar and Orissa who take no interest in Calcutta; they come here only for money and then go home"; "The Center takes from Calcutta and Bengal and gives little in return." The Bengali says he's a minority in his own city and can do nothing about the environment. Everyone has sold out to the hated Marwaris. "You should have seen it 20 years ago, Calcutta was much better, we lived better than now." Today? Today, "Calcutta is the home of endemic cholera . . ." starts the health official.

- Sitar and sirod concerts, organized in homes or pandels, and plays or poetry readings, often with an emphasis on Tagore.

- Water tanks throughout the city, open, cool, tree-lined sky reflectors that serve as community baths, animal pools, laundry centers, parks, mosquito breeders, centers of neighborhood activity. Off a main road, 15 minutes from central Calcutta, in full tropical foliage, amid only the sounds of birds, a sari-clad girl bathes in a tank in the soft filtered light of mid-morning.

- Intense, wet heat; the smell of urine in narrow streets; the smell of urine on not-so narrow streets; cool shaded streets, bustling with people, activity, color.

- Fifteen-storey office buildings rising along the Maidan, sheathed with bamboo scaffolds; and masons, hod carriers, brick carriers, and, somewhere, ochre paint.

- The Maidan, central, open, green, and filled with people at games, walking, talking, sitting, in from the village in crowded buses to get some air, buying balloons and ice cream and betel and pony rides, sleeping on the grass beneath a gol mohur and staying until late at night, every night; crowds in the open looking for relief from the heat.

You try to come to terms with new environments, however alien. Hearing or reading about wandering skin-and-bones cows is one thing; seeing them constantly is another; and being careful not to collide with one is yet another. In time it is understood that they will continue to do whatever they are doing, at the same pace, no matter how close you come in person or by auto. And so will people wash and groom themselves at street hydrants, and the people will pee where and when they must, the men different from the women only in the obviousness of their stances. Watch where you walk and be prepared, always, for beggars of all ages, who love to touch.

Dinners at homes of colleagues, with new Indian colleagues and a scattering of Europeans, offer a chance to exchange impressions, to be clever and insightful and to listen. Clubs offer a chance to swim, play tennis, eat out, let the kids run around. Clubs indeed! Whoever belonged to a club before this or would have thought about belonging to one? We find that no Indians are allowed at the Calcutta Swim Club, so, clearly, our days there are numbered. There is no racial exclusion problem at the Saturday Club. Early reading includes *The Black Hole of Calcutta* and *Behind Mud Walls*. New Bengali acquaintances will come to your house, but will rarely invite you to theirs, at least not for many months. The flimsy, crowded-together shacks of the bustees at the canal near

On a Calcutta street

Learning from Calcutta

the zoo are ever present in one's mind: the huts, and the vultures perched overhead on the bridge. Sunday afternoon teas at "Uncle Bill's" are an every-week, two- or three-hour refuge, presumably for movies for the kids, but something to do for adults as well. Bill has been doing this for years. Gafur, our first driver, is for sure stealing gas and must be fired. The British say we overpay. Dysentery comes and goes and comes again. Dropping off stool specimens at the doctor's becomes a regular activity. The first fall Hindu holidays, with their wonderful adorned clay statuary, come and go: idols paraded down to the Hooghly River, released into the muddy waters. President Kennedy is assassinated and the American colony meets in the garden of the Consul General. Our crates have been emptied. We will be here for a while. Indian acquaintances become friends. Jane starts a reading group, of great books, à la the University of Chicago. She begins to review Indian films for *The Statesman*. We are closest to an American family, the Andrades.

The second driver seems better than the first, but he has problems knowing where we're going. I give him an address and ask if he knows where that is. He says yes, but he has no idea and we never get to our destination. We talk. It's all right not to know a street and address in a district and it's better to tell me before we start out so we can figure out together where we're going. It can't be that difficult: Alipore, New Alipore, the central area, one or two other districts. Sure, continuous streets have many name changes, but we can work it out. I can call someone who knows. He agrees. "Yes, sahib." The next evening we have to go out again. I ask if he knows how to get where we're going and tell him it's okay if he doesn't know, but please tell me. "Yes, sahib." He knows where we're going. Not really. We never get there. I'm angry and fine him an amount to be taken from his salary. By the end of the month he owes me more than the salary. We're not communicating very well. I learn that it's next to impossible for him to admit he doesn't know something that maybe he should know.

The offices of the Calcutta Metropolitan Planning Organization where I work are in an old house near the Writers Building, a large and famous old brick structure where British bureaucracy holed out. We will be moving to new headquarters when a new office building is completed. I spend some days reading papers about Calcutta, the research being done, a plan prepared for New Delhi by the team that we are replacing. I try to see the city and its surrounds by walking and by driving to the outlying areas. Walking can be difficult if only because of the constancy of beggars. Will it be possible to get to know, really know, the vast area outside the city; two long strips of developed (if it can be called "developed") and developing land along the Hooghly River, the "high" land that is less prone to flooding, and the large bulge of urbanization that is Calcutta, stretching to the northeast and Dum Dum Airport? Not far to the east, on lower land, is East Pakistan, soon to become Bangladesh.

There are new Western colleagues, members of the "team," to get to know and experts in public health infrastructures, who are not part of the Ford

Foundation group. Most important, there are our Indian counterparts, many of them, to meet and to know. One wants to feel one's way, slowly. A way to do that is in meetings held to discuss myriad subjects: cholera, water salinization, sewage issues, road systems, the port and hindrances to navigation, a new port, Haldia, at the Bay of Bengal, not so far away, draining the "Salt Lake" to the east for new housing, a new community, roadway projects to connect Calcutta with the north and west. The hot item seems to be a proposal for a new, second bridge over the river, not too far from the first, that will land in the Maidan, Calcutta's one large central open space: shades of Pittsburgh, where the highway builders seemed always to pick public land, often open space, for their freeway projects. The new bridge seems to be favored by everyone around the table – World Bank people, other aid agencies, the Calcutta–Bengali officials, national representatives, engineers. But there is a minor problem to be solved and so a "sign-off" is postponed for another meeting to take place in a week or two. The issue may be over how high the bridge must be: on the one hand, the river is silting and each year the ships that can get to Calcutta are smaller. Then, too, there is the question of the Farrakah Barrage, a project that would direct more water from the Ganges River to the Hooghly, thereby reducing the silt, with implications for possible ship sizes that can be handled. But this idea is strongly opposed by the Pakistan government and will not be settled soon, so the bridge question may move forward without the barrage as a possibility. Later we would meet, socially, the English technician who was under special appointment to the Indian government and who was in charge of dredging the river. The plans were of no concern to him. His work would continue. Decisions weren't always fast coming.

There is talk of an Interim General Plan as a vehicle to focus the many studies that are going on, perhaps a way to relate them to each other. The studies are along disciplinary lines, not related to comprehensive planning. There are many discussions about new base maps that are in preparation, about map scales and appropriate levels of detail, and about measuring how land is used. And there is much talk about the new port in Haldia, and how to plan for it.

I didn't really know any of my Ford colleagues. Our leader, Jack Robin, was once an aide to Dave Lawrence when he was Mayor of Pittsburgh and later when he became Governor of Pennsylvania. Robin had a big hand in early redevelopment efforts in Pittsburgh; not as a planner, more as a facilitator and power broker. Preston Andrade, an architect, had played a quiet but major role in Philadelphia's Society Hill redevelopment program (and before that in the development of the first Link Trainer, to simulate flight for would-be pilots). There was another city planner who I was told would report to me, but no one, apparently, had told him as much. There would be yet another planner coming in some months. There was an economist, a lawyer, two geographers, a sociologist, a demographer, late of the U.S. Bureau of Census, an engineer, a regional planner, an architectural engineer, and a young traffic engineer working for an American firm of some importance. The only time we met as a team was on Saturday mornings in the Ford Foundation offices; short meetings that left us free to do things with our families in the late morning and afternoon. Our Indian counterparts were expected to work the full morning.

We, the consultants, tried to get to know each other. Only one, the sociologist from Wales, seemed to know anything of India. He didn't seem to have a high regard for urban planning or city planners, though. The young traffic man was concerned with developing a model that could be used to assess transportation needs and to prepare a new roadway system, not unlike the big traffic studies that were then the vogue in the U.S. Each specialist/expert appeared to be trying to get grounded in his or her area of expertise (there was only one female member of the team), making appropriate contacts with local and national counterparts, trying to get a fix on whatever seemed to be necessary to know, and, in short, getting the lay of the land. Civility was everywhere. It was never clear to me, at least for a year, what the first young city planner and then the second were doing. They weren't coming to me. Later I would come to suspect that each person hired was led to understand that, beyond being a member of the Ford team, he or she was pretty much a solo performer. Jack Robin was certainly understood to be the head man for Ford, and "Andy" Andrade was surely the chief technical professional, but that was as far as the organization seemed to go.

The Indian staff was formidable in size. We all made efforts to get to know as many of them as possible, particularly those who were in any way our counterparts. We met with them often. The city planners were deeply involved in achieving a good base map and in a land use study for the metropolitan district, basically to find out what was where in some accurate, systematic way; no small undertaking. Getting dependable land use data in a way that could be easily referenced was proving difficult. Another study was to get a fix on the population: how many people of what age group, sex, etc., how many refugees, numbers and trends and the like. I had some early meetings on those subjects as well as some attempts to define what a plan might be. I suggested that getting started on actually doing an Interim General Plan, even without the knowledge they were looking for, might be a good way of getting something produced – a point of departure, if nothing else. If done in a straightforward, unsophisticated way, it might be the fastest means to find out what was really needed.

I remember, early on, coming to understand that we had communication problems. I would leave a meeting thinking there was a clear understanding of a problem or a challenge, or an assignment of something to be done, only to find out later that we had misunderstood each other. The English words and phrases that meant one thing to me often seemed to mean something else to a counterpart professional. Maybe it was the context of the discussion that caused the problem, or maybe the way the words came out, the inflections. I took to writing, hoping to communicate that way, rather than with the spoken word. I asked Ford colleagues to review my writing, to be sure I was clear. They did. They understood. But the communication problems with Indian colleagues persisted. A mystery.

There were many meetings. Government bigwigs from Delhi and the U.S. visited. World health experts came, as did engineers, water experts, transportation people, housing people. Lots of people. At these meetings, P.C. Bose, the chief professional of Calcutta's Metropolitan Planning Organization, our hosts, would usually give a talk about Calcutta. At some point he would remark that the city was the world center of cholera, and then he would give some statistics about the number of daily cases.

There were more meetings about the bridge and one came to a conclusion that the decision to build was not imminent. There was always at least one more factor to be discussed or reconsidered. At one point I spent some time considering the road pattern that would be necessary to get traffic on and off a new bridge. Doing that without creating major physical disruptions on the Maidan would not be easy. In time, some of us would make bets on if and when the bridge would be built. To this day I am owed a high-priced dinner by one of the consultants. The bridge is there now, but it came late enough to win me the bet.

I was asked one day how many people would be needed to prepare a plan for a medium-sized city north of Calcutta, the site of a recent steel-mill project. After getting half answers or no answers to questions like what kind of plan was desired, when the plan was to be completed, how much detail was expected, and after taking a trip, by private Ford Foundation plane, to the area and being shown the site, I spent a few days on the task. I came up with a need for fewer than ten people and then doubled my assessment to take into consideration that they seemed to require more people to do jobs than I was accustomed to. There followed a meeting, the purpose of which was to review a proposed employment list and consequent budget that had been prepared for doing the job. There were people from Delhi and West Bengal State, as well as the Calcutta Metropolitan Planning Organization (CMPO) policy and staff people. I hadn't had any reactions after submitting my estimate. It was only when I got to that meeting that I found out that the proposed staffing was for well over 100 people! I figured I'd best just listen and try to keep my mouth shut. At one point I saw that one blueprint operator and two blueprint operator helpers were listed. I hadn't proposed any, figuring that there wouldn't be much need for blueprinting and that it would be easy to arrange with the steel-mill people to do the occasional service. Asking why two helpers were needed for one operator, I was advised that helpers got sick more often than operators. I resolved again to keep my mouth shut. Later, someone (not me, I had stopped looking) noticed that there were nine surveyors and 13 surveyors' helpers. Why the difference? There were either too many helpers or not enough surveyors. I couldn't resist saying that it was obvious that helpers fell ill more often than surveyors. General Chakravarti, the titular head of CMPO, gave me a withering look and I sensed that our relations from then on were a bit strained.

Mention was made, sporadically, of a small new-town development at the northern edge of the Calcutta Metropolitan District: Kalyani. P.C. Bose spoke highly of it. I drove there one day, to find an almost completely uninhabited town (1,000 people) of many small homes; most, if not all in the form of single-family structures on small parcels. Ebenezer Howard and his early English new towns came to mind, but Kalyani was vacant. A strange experience: all those finished houses and a just-completed sewage treatment plant with a capacity to serve 200,000 people, but nothing else there. It was quite distant from Calcutta. There seemed to be no job opportunities either nearby or as part of the development, making this an isolated, difficult-to-reach, uninhabited town.

There were meetings and more meetings about the bridge. A decision on its construction, apparently so close at the first meeting I attended, now seemed increasingly remote. I continued to focus on the matter of getting to and from a new high bridge on the Calcutta side, in the Maidan. I didn't see an easy out, one that would not damage this quite wonderful, historic central open space. The solution lay elsewhere, I thought, perhaps with Kalyani. Why bring all the truck traffic down the west side of the Hooghly River from the north and west, and then, once over the river and into congested Calcutta, send much of it back north along the river, or northeast toward Dum Dum Airport, areas of industry? Why not build a simple pontoon bridge up north, near Kalyani, something the Indian army engineers could do very easily? This would certainly be much cheaper than the contemplated bridge, and would bring the trucks and other traffic more directly to where much of it was heading already. It was a low-tech solution. Kalyani would be accessible, too. Maybe people would be more willing to move there, and more quickly. The idea went nowhere. I don't even remember receiving a response. Maybe the idea and anticipation of a new bridge were too far along to be reconsidered. Maybe my idea was thought to be too stupid to merit a response. In the end, before leaving Calcutta almost two years later, I made those bets as to when the bridge might be completed.

We had evening get-togethers with our Indian colleagues. The thought was that more informal connections between us would help in understanding and in day-to-day communication. The meetings had to be at one of the consultants' homes. I came to learn that the Marwaris, the business people in Calcutta, originally from western India, were intensely disliked. I would learn, too, that if one scratched the surface just a bit, the gulf between our largely Hindu hosts and Muslims was huge. I was to find at the office that one of our colleagues was opposed to our taking pictures in bustees because he felt we would use them to make fun of Indians. If we ever talked of substantive city planning issues, I don't recall them. Almost none of the Indian professionals were city planners in the sense of background or experience in doing plans for urban physical environments. For the most part, they were sociologists, economists, geographers, architects, and engineers. In that, they were the same as the Ford consultant team. And, like the consultants, there was a separation between the planners concerned primarily with the physical arrangement of existing and future metropolitan areas and those primarily interested in socio-economic matters; each, perhaps, saw little connection between what he (most of the CMPO staff, like ours, were men) thought important and the others' concerns. The evening meetings never became regular events; after a while, they ceased altogether. I looked for some semblance of organizational structure to evolve or be arranged by Robin and Andrade, but that didn't happen. The land use studies being done by the planning staff were slow in coming. The population information and projections seemed open to doubt.

On questions of what was where, there was one person to talk to: Chinmoy Mazumdar. As opposed to just about everyone else in the office, Chinmoy actually spent many hours in the field, on a motorbike, getting to know the Calcutta metropolitan area. He knew the land, the people, and the uses of the land. I would come to spend more and more time with Chinmoy. To him, this was more than a job: it was terribly important work. He would spend weekends out in the field, getting to know the places where he was working. From time to time we went on field trips together; part of my never-ending efforts to get a better sense of what was there, how land and people met. But Chinmoy, it seemed, was a bit outspoken and was not beloved by the office hierarchy.

Many meetings had to do with Haldia, the new port-to-be. I came up with an outline for a plan that didn't overly please General Chakravarti, though B.M. Bhuta, my counterpart, approved. On short notice staff were told it would be necessary to present work on Haldia to someone from the United Nations Special Fund. That sort of requirement often came up: how to spend unused Second (National) Plan funds, on priority transportation projects, for example, or a timetable for a plan to be presented to some visiting group or other.

At some point in that first year, or even first six months, I began to think about the matter of basic information I had been taught (and had accepted) as being essential to doing city planning: how many people of different ages there were and how the population was changing; the uses of land, what was where; jobs and categories of employment; housing conditions, amounts, and prices; people's incomes; traffic conditions and amounts and changes, mostly expected growth; and much more information like that. We wanted to know more than what existed: we wanted to know what we might expect in the future so that we could plan for it. Inevitably, the projections were based in large measure on trends, knowing what was changing and how, and the pace of change. We needed information about the past as well as the present, to gain an idea of rates of change. Here, in Calcutta, there was a lot that we didn't know and weren't likely to know, especially about the past. Historic data, especially demographic and economic, just was not there, except in hearsay.

As important, maybe more so, the projections would be based on certain assumptions: there would be no war and no economic depression; no famine; no major natural catastrophe, like a flood or an earthquake; no mass emigration or immigration; no radical change in governance; no new pestilence; no major economic leap forward; and so on. But how much sense did that make? At least some, perhaps all of those conditions had happened before and would likely happen again. So what was the basis of a plan to be? Maybe natural factors and the natures of settlement patterns of people on the land were as (or more) important for doing a plan concerned with a basic physical structure of the metropolitan region than the socio-economic data and projections. Maybe a physical framework that could best accommodate a variety of growth and change scenarios, one that respected basic land forms and water levels, would be a major accomplishment, a foundation upon which to build.

More troublesome and thought provoking, at least to me, was an extension of this thinking about predictability to "home," the U.S., where I had and likely would work. Were the assumptions any more valid in the U.S. or Europe, the developed world, than here in developing India, or so many other places? No wars? How many U.S. wars had there been since World War II? At least Korea and Vietnam; two in 20 years. And should one also count the Cold War? What of Indian wars with China and Pakistan? No inflation or recession or other economic downturns or unanticipated upturns? No tornado or hurricane or earthquake or flood to devastate local communities, if not the whole country? Wasn't the unexpected as likely to happen as the expected, even in the U.S.?

In time, these thoughts, prodded by new experiences in India, would change the way I approached city planning at home. But I shouldn't have had to travel to India to learn that lesson.

On Saturday, January 11, I took our cook-bearer, Mamud, to New Market. Usually Mamud makes this trip alone at about four or five in the morning, but Friday evening he informed us that he would not go shopping because of the potential danger to a Muslim in the market area. I had heard that afternoon that there were some disturbances between Hindus and Muslims in various parts of the city, but hadn't paid much attention. A young Hindu colleague had been damning all Muslims that morning, but then he'd also been damning most foreigners at the same time and I had put it down to a temporary bad mood. Truth is that I didn't know why there were riots, except for some rumors that Muslims in East Pakistan were giving the Hindus there a bad time. So when Mamud told me he wouldn't go shopping, I understood but wasn't overly concerned. I told him that I would drive him there after breakfast, as the mass-transit vehicles were particular targets for rioters when they put their minds to it.

The trip to New Market was uneventful; not as many cars or people on the road as usual, but otherwise quite normal. But when we got to Lindsay Street, it was apparent that something was different: the street and square in front of the market is usually a frantic, bustling place on Saturday mornings – every type of vehicle invented since the wheel, shoppers of every race and economic class, bearers shouting for your attention, beggars of every age and sex, hawkers – but today there was only a fragment of activity. I asked the driver, Babu Rao, to park the car and then accompanied Mamud on his rounds. First we stopped at Kevanter's, one of the few places in Calcutta where pasteurized milk could be purchased. Next we crossed into the produce and meat sections of New Market. Mamud walked at a brisk pace, so it was difficult to keep up with him. We saw at once that the meat section was closed. Row upon row of tables and stalls, usually laden with meat, dripping blood and surrounded by flies and people, were empty. The butchers are almost all Muslims and weren't about to do business this day. The fish market was closed and empty, too. We found some activity in the produce section and I followed Mamud between the stalls, looking, bargaining, feeling, and ultimately picking every fruit and vegetable himself. If there was tension all around, Mamud appeared unaware of it now; his only concern was quality at a good price. Physically the area was much the same as usual – fewer people, perhaps, more Western ladies because their cooks couldn't shop, but otherwise normal. I made the most of the opportunity to take some pictures, and no one paid any particular attention. We moved on to the poultry market, and Mamud must have felt ten live chickens and fifty eggs before he picked the ones he wanted.

Next was bread, but most of these shops were either too far away or closed. Then I remembered Nahoum's, a Jewish bakery that was fairly close by (excellent bread and pastries, but no rye bread because there is no rye flour). It was about one-third boarded up but was still open, albeit with limited stock. Between choosing bread and talking about the riots with one of the owners, I was only remotely aware of the noise increasing around us. First some shouting from somewhere to my right. Then people running. There was a low rumble of noise that grew in intensity and pitch as it got closer. My immediate reaction was to tell Mamud to get down. But he had disappeared. He had gone out of the shop to see the action. I stepped out and pulled the smiling cook-bearer inside. Within five or ten seconds that inefficient-looking shop was completely boarded up. An increase in activity outside and five more seconds would have found it closed tight. We heard a great deal of shouting and saw people running past but no more than that.

After a few minutes everything had quietened down and we threaded our way between the now totally boarded-up stalls to the main roadway. If there had been one-third the usual activity on Lindsay Street when we entered, there was now one-tenth and the emptiness was oppressive. Police and military personnel stood in groups along the street. Our car was gone. I was wondering what to do, but moments later I saw the car cruising toward us from Chowringhee Road. Babu Rao explained that at the first sign of riot he had left. But he had been circling the area ever since, waiting for us to turn up. We drove home, thinking nothing much had happened.

Saturday afternoon was like most others in Calcutta. Jane and the children went to the Saturday Club for tea with the family of a friend while the friend and I sat around and talked shop. Apparently the Muslims blame the Hindus for stealing a hair of the Prophet from a shrine in Kashmir. We heard that Muslim persecution of Hindus in East Pakistan had touched off the retaliatory actions in Calcutta. There were conflicting stories of killings and numbers of rioters and police injured, and comparisons with earlier communal riots, especially those that reached Calcutta at independence. We couldn't help thinking that people in America probably knew more about what was going on than we did. Then, too, because news from Calcutta is not normally prominent in the U.S. press, any news might be blown out of proportion.

Sunday was largely uneventful for us. We heard conflicting stories of riots and killings and the burning of Muslim bustees by Hindus and vice versa. We heard of police brutality or inactivity, of Hindu policemen standing by as Muslims were beaten. We heard of looting and beatings, but for once not of the streetcar burnings that happen with regularity during riots. We heard of troops and curfews and food shortages, and of youth groups made up of Muslims and Hindus who, with no regard for personal safety, worked to restore order and help the unprotected and injured. We heard all these things but could verify little. Coverage of such happenings in local papers can be scant or non-existent. Some have a policy of purposely not reporting such events for fear of spreading the trouble.

On Sunday morning, we passed the annual horse show of the Indian Society of Equitation and Horsemastership held at the racecourse in the Maidan. For a fleeting moment I saw a picture that was then lost as we moved on: in the foreground there were children on horses – British, other Westerners, and Indians – going through the disciplined exercises as their parents looked on proudly; in the middle ground, about a quarter-mile away, stood the Victoria Memorial, the splendidly white marble monument to the British Raj; and in the background, some one or two miles distant, rose black smoke from a burning slum set alight by rioters in the Sealdah Railway Station area.

On Sunday night, we were as much in the dark as before. News, via a friend, via the U.S. Consul (so perhaps inaccurate), was that there would probably not be any general outbreak of rioting. Apparently the government had worked much faster than in the massacres of 1946 and 1947, and had sent adequate troops to handle the situation. Schools and many market areas would be closed. We were to stay off the streets at night if possible, and keep out of the troubled areas – the bustees, university areas, and some other fairly isolated trouble spots – and abide by police restrictions in the areas where we lived. Most of the violence was directed against property rather than people.

Slowly, I had been coming to a conclusion that not far under the calm, civil, day-to-day relationships between people of different religious, regions of birth, and race, there might well be deep dislikes, even hatreds, and that this might be so among highly educated, sophisticated professionals. The riots reinforced that conclusion.

At one corner of our dining-room table, indented into the clear varnish, there was a small circular pattern, maybe four inches in diameter, an indent of hair. After spotting this intrusion in the tabletop, it took a few days to understand what that pattern was and how it got there. It had been necessary to order new furniture upon arriving in Calcutta and it had to be made: sofas, chairs, desks, bookcases, various tables, including the dining-room table. It arrived piece by piece over a period of maybe three or four weeks, rather quickly I thought. We had asked for a rubbed oil finish for the table, but that was not to be, perhaps through mis-communication. The delivery, especially of the large, flat pieces, was often by hand, or rather by head. Hand- or animal-drawn carts were normal means of delivery, small trucks less frequent, but groups of men, carrying something together, the item resting on their heads, was very common. That, it seemed clear to me, was the way our table had arrived: four men, one at each corner of the upside-down table, had carried it from somewhere in central Calcutta, through the Maidan and up New Alipore Road to our home. But the varnish hadn't yet fully dried and the circular pads worn on the heads of the bearers, to cushion them against the table, hadn't quite covered the head of one of the bearers, so his hair pattern was printed into the corner of the table. There were no similar patterns at the other three corners; only this one, next to the place where I usually sat. I could and did look at that hair pattern twice each day, imagining four men carrying that table through Calcutta.

In going to India, my assumption – and I was never advised otherwise – had been that we were to be advisors to an Indian staff; that the local staff were to prepare the plan and that we would advise on organizational, research, and analysis matters, and provide technical knowledge and ideas, in my case ideas for alternative future physical arrangements of the developed environment, to achieve locally determined objectives, mostly having to do with efficiency and social progress, always respectful of the natural environment. In truth, I suspect I have just stated the assumption more clearly than was ever expressed at the time. The trouble was that as time passed it became increas-ingly clear that we, the Ford Foundation group, had no organizational structure of our own, let alone any clear policy guide as to what might be the outcomes of our being there.

Not to be outdone, as near as I could tell, the staff of the CMPO was non-arranged in similar fashion. We were an assemblage of individuals, acting as such, and the CMPO's "organization," beyond the somewhat loose land use planning group headed by B.M. Bhuta, was unknown to me. I was intent on not doing a plan myself or on being the leader–director of a plan with subservient Indian staff. In my mind that would not be kosher. I was not there to be a colonialist. Certainly local, intelligent, professional people would know better than I what physical organizations made most sense, at various physical scales, as responses to local socio-economic history, culture, future. In this case, what, exactly, constituted "local" was something to consider. It might or might not be Indian. For sure, it meant Bengali, which didn't always coincide with char-acteristics, values, and ways of thinking shared by other – non-Bengali – people of the subcontinent. In retrospect, of course, the same would be true of people of the U.S. East, Midwest, South, Northern Plains, Southwest, California, and San Francisco Bay Area.

I was coming to know, or think, that Bengalis might well come into the world, first day, as full-fledged attorneys–debaters, eager to argue any side of an issue and with an amazing ability to come up with or respond to an idea or proposal and explain why that proposal would not work simultaneously, not sequentially. It was a magnificent, if somewhat trying, quality for this Midwestern American to understand. Though I knew very little at the time about university cultures, I wondered and have wondered since if Bengalis are, inherently, the perfect academics. One sensed that the non-Bengali professionals were having communication problems themselves within the CMPO team. In any case, the physical planning staff did not appear to be working according to any schedule, outline, or organizational structure; nor did it appear that the whole of CMPO was. If there were a plan or program, I was having no luck in determining its nature. Nor was I successful in generating one, either for the CMPO staff with whom I was concerned or for the Ford team. I began to think that the problem might be mine alone; that this was a new working situation, one with which I had no experience. I contemplated that maybe I needed to wait; that things would shake themselves out and that in time I would come to understand and be useful.

This is not to say that I wasn't busy or involved in the comings and goings of the CMPO. My engagement calendars and notes are full of meetings to discuss the boundaries of the district for mapping purposes (months and months after the mapping had started), meetings about Haldia (even an admonition to myself to "Do Haldia Sketch Planning"), seeing this person or that to get data, innumerable meetings about work programming or organization alternatives, conferences with visitors, reviewing outlines, discussions about open space and recreation planning, cost estimating, setting priorities for the fourth five-year plan, even (on July 26, 1964, after almost a year) a note to prepare a summary CMPO approach for Haldia, including how it might be planned, what the planning should include, and an organizational framework. According to Jack Robin, at a staff meeting, the Ford Foundation people in New York were very happy with the progress in Calcutta. There had been a report about us on U.S. television; everything was great, and more visitors would be coming.

We moved to new offices at the end of July 1964.

On August 15, almost one year after arriving in Calcutta, I was rushed to hospital – actually the Woodlands Nursing Home – to be operated on for an appendix that was about to burst. Appendectomies, it seemed, were reasonably common for Westerners. Some wise old hand had advised me not to have an operation in Calcutta: the operation would be successful but I would die of post-operative infection. Nevertheless, an about-to-burst appendix would not wait. One or two days after the event a small contingent of the CMPO staff came to the nursing home. They were looking for advice on how to proceed on something or other, and I was able to help them. Was this some major breakthrough?

I suspect not. But, looking back, there must have been something that I and we were doing that made me a somewhat integral part of the CMPO planning effort.

One member of the Ford team, Collin Rosser, seemed to know India well. In discussions he seemed to have little use for city planners, due to an apparent belief that as a group we were enthralled with large-scale clearance of so-called slums, with consequent dislocation of untold numbers of poor people, to be replaced by ill-conceived projects that would in any case not rehouse those who had been displaced or their like. He seemed not to want to hear that not all of us were clearance-and-rebuild folks; that keeping and rehabilitating substandard areas, and finding vacant sites for new housing, especially for the neediest, was central to our concerns. Also, while we might hold that the physical environment did indeed influence, at least in some small part, how people might act – they try to wear warm clothes when it is cold, use umbrellas when it rains, walk in any available shade when it is hot, shade that has sometimes been planned – we were not all full-fledged physical determinists, as that phrase was pejoratively used. It was not always easy to talk with Collin.

He was working, and would continue to work over an extended period, on what would come to be called a "bustee improvement program." The bustees were among the most difficult of Calcutta's (indeed India's) housing areas, made up of shacks constructed of a wide variety of catch-as-catch-can materials but with a fair amount of clay walls and corrugated-metal roofs. They might or might not have electricity (usually not) and certainly had no individual water taps or sewer connections or latrines. A water tap here, a latrine there; these were communal in nature. The shacks or huts were extremely close together, lined along unpaved paths that might be three feet wide, without lighting. There might well be a "tank" somewhere amid the development, used for bathing and also for animals, particularly water buffalo. However bad and unhealthy the bustees were generally, they were worse during the monsoon rains. Nevertheless, I spent time walking in the bustee near the Hooghly River and the Howrah Bridge, and the one between central Calcutta and New Alipore, abutting the zoo, and was continually amazed, not at the squalor and poverty, but at the relative cleanliness, given the crowding, the construction, and, most of all, the lack of utilities.

In these environments, Rosser's would-be program, one that would become a reality, was not to do away with the bustees, but to improve them: new latrines and water-tap stations of simple, easily produced designs, well placed; paving for the paths; a few overhead lights; precast and standardized parts. It all sounds so simple, but its execution would take a couple of years to get under way. In the end, the program may have been the most successful, tangible evidence of the Ford team's stay, and it would be exported to other Indian cities.

Fairly early on, I decided to visit Bombay, now Mumbai, to see what the other major commercial, port city of India was like. To me, it was a wonderfully alive, even reasonably ordered city, made attractive by the particular ornate grandness of the designs of major civic buildings. Walking around the city was fairly easy and one didn't get the sense of overwhelming poverty that was everywhere in Calcutta. Food that you wouldn't come close to in Calcutta seemed almost consumable in Bombay. There wasn't the sense of decay that was everywhere in Calcutta. The waterside setting helped. At about that time I read Arthur Koestler's *The Lotus and the Robot*. He describes landing in Bombay and the poverty, shacks, street dwellers, hunger, and dirt that assault the senses. He expresses a kind of hopelessness. His perceptions and reactions were so different from mine. Trying to understand, it occurred to me that he had arrived from Switzerland; I had come from Calcutta.

Time passes. Daily lives are led. Amy and Matthew go to school every morning, to Loretto House, where the nuns have promised not to give them religious training, but seem not to be able to resist the temptation. I drop them off on many mornings. Matthew is not at all happy at the school and sometimes I have trouble getting him to enter. Once inside, the class will be taken to morning prayers, which the nuns had promised that our children would be spared. On the way to prayers, Matthew walked at the end of the line of his classmates, disappeared behind a large column as they passed, or went into the lavatory, waited for the class to return, then joined the end of the line on its way back to class. Not bad for a six-year-old.

Jane made some friends, with two local ladies in particular, and was increasingly active in film reviews. We were welcomed on the set of a Satyajit Ray film, to watch the great director at work. We entertained and were entertained on many evenings. Often, I would meet the family at the Saturday Club in the late afternoon, and play with the kids in the pool before tea. All the children were cared for by a nanny. The Calcutta Swim Club was a Sunday morning destination until, one evening, there was a meeting about whether to admit Indians. Jane attended. The next day we sent in our resignation from the club. We visited the Andrades, played badminton in their yard. Amy and Matthew took riding lessons at the Calcutta Society of Equitatian and Horsemastership. Sundays were often problems: what to do? The best times were early evenings, before dinner, when I could play with the kids on our bed.

Recording and depicting Calcutta became important for me. That was better done on black-and -white film than on Kodachrome slides, where the color too easily distracted from the subject or content. Much time was spent walking and driving around the city and surrounds, looking and taking pictures. One Saturday morning there was a blind man, with leprosy, begging. He sat on his heels. Behind him, painted on a wall, were political slogans, rubbed out, but not completely. There was a cruciform shape to the wall. The man was blind, with leprosy; political slogans come and go; the man's ass does not touch the ground.

Mamud, the cook-bearer, had a wonderful twinkle in his eye. He was critical of my purchases. Whenever I bought something he would ask how much I paid. Whatever I told him, even if I lied, he would say, "Too much, sahib, too much." One evening a rug salesman came, by appointment, with many, many

Kashmiri carpets for sale. Mamud watched the proceedings from behind the dining-room door; good entertainment for him and Bassant, the sweeper. Whenever Mamud sensed that we might be ready to buy something he called me from the doorway and advised me that the price was too high. After this had happened four or five times, the rug man was furious and yelled at Mamud. We told the rug man to leave.

One night our downstairs neighbor knocked on the door. Mamud was with him. The neighbor had found the cook-bearer with some of our canned food-stuffs, and said, almost insisted, that we should fire him. I said I'd handle it. Mamud looked terrible and was contrite. Later, I had reason to believe that he had taken food again and some liquor. He denied it. I was angry with him and showed it. That week, we were invited to go to an evening party and I decided to wear a dhoti, draped and creased properly, as Mamud knew how to do. We reached the hosts' doorway, took one step inside, and the dhoti came undone. I grasped. Mamud's revenge!

At a Ford staff meeting in early September, we were informed that important central government people would be coming the next day and that they expected a series of conferences to review position papers. World Bank people would be there as well, with interest in the bridge, Haldia, and water supply. Then, too, Chester Bowles, the U.S. Ambassador to India, was determined to get a Calcutta improvement program going, a seven-year program, and wanted to know what could be achieved in two years. A big question was who would prepare the position papers and who would do the plans. B.M. Bhuta told us his problems. Jarna Roy, a sociologist, came to me with papers to be reviewed, but they had little to do with a possible plan for Calcutta.

The central government people came and left. I wasn't in the meetings with them and didn't know what they were told. Perhaps I was out of the loop; if there was a loop. Nothing seemed to change in either the CMPO group or the Ford group. I still didn't know what the two young Ford planners were doing and wondered why I wasn't kept aware. By mid-October it was being suggested that the Ford team should take over the Calcutta Metropolitan District planning. In early November we were still discussing a goals paper with Bhuta. A bridge decision was still pending: should it be 135 feet or 125 feet high?

Before I decided to go to Calcutta, a young Indian planner, Rabindrah Gupta, had come to work at the office in Pittsburgh. He was fresh from graduate school at Harvard, where, not wealthy, he had done all kinds of jobs, including cleaning lavatories, to make ends meet. We got to know each other and were on our way to becoming friends. He was modestly positive about our move to Calcutta, but could not tell us much about the city, having spent his life in or near Delhi. At some point, early in our second Calcutta year, he turned up, looking for work at the CMPO. Our being there, in Calcutta, may have had something to do with his return to India.

Gupta had a hard time readjusting to India and adjusting to Calcutta. The "culture shock" he had experienced during his first months in Boston was matched, maybe surpassed, by his first weeks "home." Without knowing it, he had become accustomed to living in the West, with so many things taken for granted, simple things like clean water out of taps that didn't require boiling before drinking, general sanitation, ease of movement, uncrowded streets, space, and general well-to-do-ness. There were also daily living conditions in Calcutta (as well as Delhi) that perhaps he had never seen, or allowed himself to be aware of, that were as shocking to him as they had been to us at first. I recall him ordering meat in a restaurant and eating meat in our house, although there were alternatives: it seemed an act of defiance, as if to say, "I ate meat in America and I like it. I'm not going to stop now, even if my upbringing was not to do so." He, too, wasn't quite sure of what he was to do at the CMPO. He lived at the home of a family member who was a senior law enforcement officer, and whose house was within the police compound. This was most difficult for Gupta, because he could hear the unsavory sounds of arrests at night, during what must have been very forceful interrogations. He spent time with us, not sleeping at our place, but eating some meals and going home late. He began to wonder if returning to India had been a mistake and to think about emigrating, perhaps to Canada.

One Saturday night Gupta, Jane and I went to a movie house on a central area upscale street off Chowringhee. The movie over, we walked out in the crowd and I was careful to walk in the street, where there was space, not up against the buildings. At some point I simultaneously sensed and glimpsed something and, in an instantaneous, reflexive action, grabbed a hand that was in Gupta's shirt pocket: a pickpocket in action. I clutched the wrist as tight as I could and began to twist it. Whatever was in the hand dropped for Gupta to recapture, and I kept twisting. People began to look. I felt that something, the arm, was about to break or pop out of its socket. What was I doing? I threw it away: arm attached to body. The whole episode could not have taken more than three or four seconds. Adrenaline works fast. Would that the reflexes worked so fast on occasions in Rome, many years later, when twice I had my pocket picked on buses. My Italian friends get a kick out of that. But in Calcutta, that night, Gupta was ashamed and depressed: in his own country a Westerner – a friend, but a Westerner nonetheless – knew the ropes better than he.

In the years to follow, Gupta would indeed go to Canada and, later, to the United States. In 2004 a newspaper carried a small article and a picture of him at the Library of Congress, where he looked after the nation-founding papers and perhaps explained them to visitors.

The shape is unmistakable: a baby grand piano. It is in the street, just off center, and it is moving, slowly. There is room for cars, lorries, carts, and people to pass it: people alone on the side closest to the buildings, but they must crowd past it, with cars and people on the other side. No one seems to pay much attention to the beautifully polished black instrument, but from directly above, perhaps some 30 feet, it is hard to tell if passers-by find the piano an incongruous sight in their comings and goings. A cow walks by, slowly, uninterested. From directly overhead a piano seems particularly strange on a street near the center of Calcutta, with all that activity, normal Calcutta street activity, around it. The baby grand stops. A man disappears under it. Another emerges. The sequence is repeated: a man goes under, another comes out; nine or ten times. Then the piano is moving again, slowly but steadily. A baby grand piano, shiny, black, elegant, weaving its way through the crowded streets of Calcutta.

The view changes and one is reminded almost immediately of the famous painting by Piero della Francesca hanging in Arezzo, the one with all the horses and warriors and so many horses' legs that you wonder if there are more or fewer than four times the number of horses' heads. It isn't easy to tell which legs belong to which heads. Here, though, it is men's legs, so many of them, bare and glistening with sweat, with loosely draped light cloth – gray, once white – that begins at the knees or slightly above, and all of the legs are moving in unison, from left to right. The movement makes it impossible to count the number of legs. The focus moves downward, to the calves, ankles, and feet; many feet, shades of brown, half of them picking up together in Radio City Hall Rockettes chorus-line precision, while the other half land. They attach to sandals: some of leather with a strap across the foot and a loop for the big toe; others, the majority, cut-outs, made from the treads of old tires. They march along together, the feet and legs, half up, half down. There is considerable background noise: a low rumbling sound through which comes a whistle, horns, voices. Focus moves upward, pauses at the legs, then continues to torsos, most bare, a few covered with very light cloth, much more sweat, and on to necks and chins, firmly set, moving forward. Then there are heads: ten, maybe. Only the heads. Faces are taut, fixed, looking straight ahead, jaws set. Straight mouths, dark visages, sweat. On each head there is a roll of cloth, a pad, between head and piano. Some pads are thicker than others, to account for height differences. Ten men carry the baby grand on their heads. Slowly, again, the men's faces are in view, close up, grim, mouths down at the corners, expressionless, determined, dark brows, eyes straight ahead, backs ramrod straight, arms swinging in unison, wet body cloths, knees and legs, knees and legs, feet, 20 feet.

The piano moves through the city, through crowded streets, mostly narrow, turns a corner, many people, city noises, voices, faintly a tune, a herd of goats divides to let the piano pass, on and on, through the streets. Bearers are replaced, one by one, in the procession. New faces, new bodies, new legs, new sweat, but the picture is the same. Then something changes; not just the tune, now a bit louder. There are three more heads, six more legs. Each of these heads, too, has a cloth pad upon which is resting the underside of a horizontal surface; but not the underside of the piano. The music increases in volume, a Cole Porter tune. From directly above, the focus is once again on the baby grand, not all of it, just a close-up of the top, which is now propped open; clearly the source of "Just One of Those Things." The view moves slowly in the direction of the keyboard, now also open, to long, thin fingers working over the keys, and then to a slight, elegant, black-haired Western man in a tuxedo, sitting on a piano bench and playing, playing as the baby grand moves on, through the streets – just one of those things. Now, people watch, some even smile, some shake their heads, others look down from windows, their heads in the direction of the music. A passing cow, unmoved, continues on its path.

Well into our second year, I decided to do a plan for physical growth and development of the Calcutta Metropolitan Area; call it a structural plan. Given my predisposition not to lead the drafting of a plan, certainly not to impose my thoughts or visions on the host community, but more to offer whatever knowledge I might have as just one part of a team, this was a big decision, one that was both evolving and consciously directed while being personally troubling; but not enough to refrain from doing it.

As a planner–designer of urban physical developments, at whatever scale, I regularly sketched ideas that responded to the physical environment itself – land forms, climate, water, what was already built – as well as social, economic, and governmental forces at work or likely to be such. The sketches, often nothing more than simple diagrams, were ideas of possibilities, hypotheses, assertions of a

Foraging cow

"What if . . .?" nature, to be built up, tested, considered, taken to a higher level of detail, or thrown away. As much as responding to research questions, the diagram sketches might be a basis for further research. Near-constant sketching and diagramming is what designer–planners do. It's like talking or playing with numbers or words or symbols. It is a way of communicating. I had seen none of this among my Indian colleagues and certainly none among the Ford group. Andy was more than able (in fact he had a fine hand) but that isn't what he was doing. And I had virtually given up trying to figure out what the other two Ford city planners were doing, sensing that both of them might be bent on establishing an independent international consulting company of one sort or another.

I told the small CMPO planning group my idea of what a physical framework plan might be, let them know that I was starting to work on one, and asked for input. Where should future urban development be? How should it relate to a transportation network that could somehow be kept open, not built up and then choked by squatting settlements and building intrusions? Was it even possible to think of a system of open spaces? If there were a plan, how could it be easily administered, especially at a very local, neighborhood scale? What of the high land, if any land could be called "high," and the low, often flooded, land? I gave a tentative direction or two: work that I thought should be done. A few of the staff seemed to respond positively; most seemed noncommittal, at best. Morale, none too high in the first place, seemed to decline. There was distance between me and Bhuta. I gave one staff person a piece of my mind about his work habits, explained I would have fired him if he'd worked for me. Chinmoy Mazumdar was one who did get involved, and it was a joy working with him. Young Monideep Sharma got into the mix at some point. And there was a young lady sociologist, Jharna Roy, who had real promise but seemed reluctant to speak out.

Before the end of 1964, there began to be talk and speculation among the Ford group about staying after our two-year commitments had been met. I had started in August 1963. I was fairly convinced that I would return to the U.S. but didn't say anything, had even jotted down possible conditions for staying. And now there was work to do. There is nothing like a deadline, self-imposed or not, to get one hopping.

The challenge, really quite stimulating, was to do a meaningful, useful for the future, physical plan for an area where so little about today or tomorrow was known, or could be known. Of course, when you think about it, the same could be said of the challenge of so many earlier planned cities: Philadelphia, New York, Savannah, Detroit, for example. The answer, I thought, was to come up with a basic structure of public ways combined with land to be urbanized, a structure that could allow for any number of land uses and combination of uses. The best structure seemed to be two basically lineal developments, one along each side of the river, except for the non-lineal explosion of development that characterized existing Calcutta, and for the spine that went northeast toward and beyond the airport. More detailed substructures, but never *too* detailed, would be required as well. But this was a start, at the scale of the metropolitan region.

There were days when work was fun: the new offices were a major improvement over the old ones, sketching, drawing, throwing away lots of paper, talking with Mazumdar and Andy, discussing ideas. One morning, as I wiped the drawing board with my forearm, I noticed what seemed to be dust particles. By noon I had developed a sty in one eye and another starting in the other; a malady I had never had. I took myself off to the doctor, a Welshman who was becoming an expert in tropical diseases, preparatory to returning to London, where he would be a high-priced specialist. He took one look at me, from a safe distance of about six or seven feet, and revealed that I had "spider spit," a highly contagious condition caused by excretions of a very small spider that had been frightened. Apparently, those dust particles had been the very small, scared spiders in question. Later, I must have touched my hand to my face: spider spit! Not to worry. I took a prescription to Sahib Singh's, the local pharmacy, obtained the ointment, and was better by that night.

Slowly, slowly, the local staff and I became more compatible; at least I felt that to be the case. Days were better. There was no secrecy about what I was doing. People could be involved or not, as they chose. Talking together was easier. It was a gradual change. At the time, I put it down to the possibility that what I/we were doing made sense and that tangible proposals were being developed – something to hang on to, at least a bit, or to depart from; something more than talk. Maybe the apparent unity of purpose, apparent perhaps only to me, was due simply to the passage of time: after all, we had been occupying the same space every day for more than a year. We were becoming accustomed to each other. Perhaps it had to do with the power of drawings. Over and over again, since then, I have been convinced of their importance and of the credibility accorded the person who uses the pencil or pen, as long as what is drawn is reasonable. Drawing can both transcend language and simultaneously encourage discussion. One can see what is intended by the words and openly argue, expand, create. Maybe, too, it had to do with my personal understanding that I would be leaving in August, and, having decided to engage in doing a plan, to accept responsibility for actively advocating ideas, I was being more myself.

There were many reasons for deciding to leave. For sure, I was not comfortable with the Ford team, the purpose and direction of which I never fully understood: there seemed no singleness of purpose. I didn't feel that our leader, Jack Robin, held city planning in high regard; or, for that matter, long-range or even short-range policy-making. Rather, he was more of an opportunist. Mostly, though, I was moving more and more to a conclusion that we, none of us, belonged there. We didn't really understand the historical, social, political, or economic contexts of India, West Bengal, or Calcutta, and we never would, never could. Our words to each other didn't mean the same things. "Yes" didn't mean "yes." "No" was rarely said. Put simply, I didn't think we understood the culture. Moreover, the local people, the professionals, were highly intelligent and were perfectly capable of preparing their own plan for the Calcutta area. Why, really, did they need us? We must have felt like a weight on them, a vote of no confidence by their leaders. I had never had problems of communication with colleagues before this. Perhaps it was little things like the staff person who didn't want us to take pictures of slums or poverty because he felt we would use them to make fun of Indians. To me, there was an uncomfortable sense of pre-sumptuousness behind the whole effort.

There were family-based reasons not to stay, too. The family was chang-ing: two years in the life of a two-year-old, Janet's age when we arrived, or of a five-year-old, Matt, or of a seven-year-old, Amy, is a lot. And the kids were changing. Their education was of a make-do, not a permanent, nature. Matthew had never been happy, particularly at school. Amy made do, but her friends were limited. Janet would soon be ready to start school. Her life in Calcutta was much defined by time with a nanny. Living with and becoming accustomed to nannies and servants would not last long for us. This was not my kind of life, never would be. Though we had gone on family holidays together, to Puri on the coast, we had also left the kids in Calcutta on at least one occasion, to visit Delhi, and that bothered me. In Calcutta, we saw less of them than we might in the U.S. Jane, after months of great discomfort after our arrival, had found friends, activities, and interests, mostly to do with film reviewing. At the same time, there were the first strains to our marriage; not easy to define, but I knew something was wrong. I was out of my element. While continuing to work on the plan, I began to make enquiries about job prospects in the U.S.

The plan proceeded. I thought I was becoming appropriately accepting of Indian realities – a religious building, no matter how small or recent, for example, could not be moved, even for a major road – and I was having fun devising basic structural physical frameworks that would be able to deal with unknown future development, and ways to protect new circulation improvements from becoming overrun with new, choking street-side shacks. Ideas for linear fish farms and tanks as part of urban life and at the same time as integral to a physical structure were sketched and drawn. Non-bureaucratic ways of managing and self-enforcing neighborhood plans were developed. We worked at a number of physical scales, but mostly at a physical structure for the metropolitan region. Yes, "we" began to replace "I," or at least I think it did. Relations with a small group of the Indian staff were easy and there was good feeling. There was interest and perhaps even a buying into the plan. Andy, whose desk was near mine, certainly knew what we were doing. I wish I could say the same for the other Ford consultants. In the humidity of my second monsoon season, close to departing, I put together a small mimeographed, bound copy of a draft plan for the metropolitan area of Calcutta, with text and graphics.

We are driving to work – Edgar, the driver, and me – in the light blue Ford that I have used since arriving. The morning is brilliantly sunny, the air clear, the colors sharp, the grass very green, the sky a Windsor blue and the white clouds whiter than any have a right to be. The air, the colors, the brightness can be like this after an early monsoon rain. We are driving through the Maidan as we do on so many mornings, to the office. Ahead of us the road is clear, no cars in either direction. On the other side of the road, beyond a large puddle or small lake left by last night's rain, a man is walking. He has the usual black umbrella, no use for it at the moment, carried like a walking stick. His dhoti is white, crisp like the morning, freshly ironed, a nice picture against the greens of the Maidan. Without warning, Edgar veers and catches the puddle, sending a sheet of water into the air, not so clean and sparkling after all, dousing the poor fellow on the other side. I am aghast. Edgar, smiling, comes out with, "Oh, those Indians," and speeds off. I shout at him to stop the car and when he finally does, I look back. The man is nowhere in sight. Edgar, full name Edgar Kenyon Derosaire, is Anglo-Indian. He has lasted longer than other drivers. His son has recently died and he was back at work in two days. On one occasion I managed to keep him out of jail after he had an accident when Matthew was in the car. Now, I tell Edgar he will be fired if he ever does anything like that again.

The next day we are again driving through the Maidan. The setting is the same: the brightness, the colors, the lake–puddle, the man in the crisp, white, ironed dhoti. Edgar does it again: the swerve, the car in the puddle, the sheet of water, the soaking. He simply couldn't resist. I fire him and will hire yet another driver. I had hoped not to have to do that. It won't be all that long before we leave.

What have I missed? That Edgar, born and residing his whole life in Calcutta, does not consider himself Indian, is an alien, and that I, like him and of the same Anglo roots, would understand?

The trip home was to complete a round-the-world tour that had started two years earlier from Pittsburgh: this time to Delhi, Israel, Istanbul, Athens, Nice, Paris, and Cleveland, before moving to Philadelphia, where a teaching position at the University of Pennsylvania awaited. In Nice, on the beach, we read of the riots in Los Angeles, in the Watts area. My mind went back to a trip there a few years earlier, and a drive with friends to see Simon Rodia's Watts Towers.

Driving through Watts, on local streets, can take a while: many small bungalows widely spaced; wide streets; poor but not terrible maintenance, houses and area in much better condition than the gritty brick row houses of Pittsburgh's Hill District; few people to be seen, mostly minority blacks or of Latin American roots; a low-density sprawling vastness. At some point, Jane squeezed my hand, not in passion. A while later, she asked Tom if we would soon be there, out of this area in which she felt increasingly uneasy. What, I wondered, had triggered her fear and need to get out of it? The people were fewer and the conditions, at least those that were visible, were much better than so-called slum areas of Pittsburgh or other cities we knew.

And now there were riots in Watts, soon to be followed in other U.S. cities, especially gritty cities of the East and Midwest. Why Watts? Sitting on that beach in Nice, a strange juxtaposition, I thought about it. In Watts there seemed no way out. Flat and visually endless, once in Watts you were there: no way, at least no easy way, out. In hilly Pittsburgh, in much worse and crowded immediate surroundings, there was always a way out, if only a view. One can always see and imagine oneself out. I wasn't overly surprised at those riots.

The trip also provided time to think, if only a little, about Vietnam. In India we hadn't heard much, read much, or paid much attention to the U.S. involvement there. Now I began to wonder and question. What was the U.S. doing there and what did we really know about that country?

Before going to Calcutta, people had warned us about "culture shock," the impact upon one's senses of the vast differences in standards, ways of life, ways of thinking and doing; in short, differences of cultures. They hadn't mentioned "reverse culture shock" – the constant surprises attendant to returning home after being in such a different place for two years. Most surprising was coming to understand that few people, if any, were more than superficially interested in our experiences or in knowing what Calcutta was like, or what our life had been like, or what the people were like. We were full of India, but there was no one to talk with about it. People were interested in the now of their own lives.

As if to underline that coming-home experience, soon after moving to Philadelphia, I found myself interviewed by Hugh Downs on what was then the *Today* television program, to talk about Calcutta and conditions there. I took along some pictures. I went to the network offices in New York City, was shown to a room, was asked a few questions about myself, what I had been doing in Calcutta, and about health and poverty there. Then the make-up people took over for a few minutes; mostly talcum on my shaved head. Downs, when I was taken to a seat next to him in the studio, was a vision of thick pancake make-up who did not look directly at me. A few words passed between us and then there was a break for a commercial. In the pause there was no banter between us. After the break, I recalled P.C. Bose, in Calcutta, giving cholera statistics. Back on camera, Downs wanted to know if people got accustomed to hunger. Struck silent for a moment, I eventually replied that, no, I didn't think people ever got accustomed to hunger. Hunger hurts, I said. On the train back to Philadelphia, I pondered the nature of television as a huge consumption machine. It was impossible to produce new material, constantly, interestingly, for what were then only three or four stations. The machine needed to be fed continually. For ten or so minutes, side by side with Downs, I had been its fodder. A piece of India had been consumed during that time.

So, why India? Why did I, we, decide to go to Calcutta in 1963? Good, positive answers still evade me and maybe always will. Perhaps the answer does indeed lie in being something of a sucker when asked for help for what seems to be a good cause: a desire to do good for people in a place that needs it. That's what the Ford Foundation invitation seemed to be about. On the other hand, an overly active need to be wanted might also explain such a response. Whatever the reasons, there was experience to be gained and lessons to be learned, hopefully positive.

I learned that I didn't belong in India, doing what I had been brought there to do. Nor did the Ford Foundation team belong there; not in a planning role. Neither I nor we understood the cultural environment we were working in or its relation to the physical setting; and we never would. How dare we think that we could tell our hosts what to do? At worst, we were involved, largely, in a type of colonialism without calling it that, together with, at best, intellectual professional tourism. Like it or not, our hosts were put in a subservient position, especially in relation to anything that might require funding by international agencies whose language we spoke better than they did. Moreover, the local people were totally capable of doing their own planning. In reality, I wonder how much of a distraction we were to their getting on with the job. To be sure, there were some technical matters related to sanitation, health, and engineering where outside expertise might have been needed, but the same was not true for policy-making or deciding what should go where and in what overall physical form. To know what you don't know and that you probably never will know is no small lesson. In fact, I think it is the most important lesson. It can lead to one's learning without the requirement of action, and it can lead to great caution before telling people what is best for them.

Soon after returning from India, questions about the U.S.'s role in Vietnam grew increasingly urgent. What were we doing there? Forest defoliation? What did we know of the Vietnamese? The Viet Cong? Why should we care if they were communists or socialists? If it was a matter of ideology, then shouldn't we be promoting democracy and well-being at home? If there was some necessity to be on one side or the other, were we on the wrong one? Wasn't it telling that in 1965, the year we returned to the U.S., there were race riots in Los Angeles, soon to spread across the country? What were we into in Vietnam that we didn't know anything about? After two years in India, I knew that I knew nothing about it. What did the U.S. know about Vietnam? These questions would arise again and again. Is it true that the Sunnis and the Shi'ites have been at each other tooth and nail, hatred upon hatred, for about 1,000 years in what is now Iraq? What did we, *do* we, really know about that part of the world? About Afghanistan? What would lead us to a righteous, largely unilateral war action there? At the very least, shouldn't we act only if many other peoples and countries are prepared to join with us?

A return to isolationism? Not at all. We are all in and of this world. We need to live together, and the more we know of each other, the better; travel, study, mix, by all means. Discuss. But go very slowly and with the greatest caution before even thinking you, or we, can tell people what is best for them and what they should do. And go slower still before pressuring people, economically or otherwise, to do things your, or our, way. Be suspicious of your own expertise, particularly in places about which you don't know much. For sure, some actions require fast, "stop it" reactions: racial or ethnic cleansing, systematic sexual abuse, arbitrary imprisonment, torture, the list is long. But the need for rapid response should be multinational. And if the United Nations isn't up to the job, then it should be made to be so.

In light of these conclusions, how can later, personal consulting commissions in Ahmedabad, China, Brazil, Abu Dhabi, even Canada be explained or justified? Perhaps they cannot. Rationalization can take many forms. After many years working professionally in San Francisco, teaching, researching and writing in Berkeley, and after forming a small urban design consulting firm with my wife-to-be, we were invited to Ahmedabad to help a young colleague solve a street design problem. Our jointly determined solution for C.G. Road seemed and seems to fit the bill. But were the proposal and its ensuing reality not much more than an example of exporting Western history and ways of doing things to India, yet again? How different is C.G. Road than any number of English colonial multi-way boulevards in Delhi? What would a more purely local design have produced? There is no point in trying to imagine an Indian alternative: only an Indian could do that. No Westerner could have imagined the unique step wells for which Ahmedabad is famous. Does this mean that Louis Kahn's much-admired Indian Institute of Management, also in Ahmedabad, has no place there? To this Western observer it seems both to fit with its context and to avoid shouting "Louis Kahn" or international style or any other period or geography. But I may not be correct. Again, Indian people would be better judges. Does Classic Revival or Gothic belong in the U.S.? Many would hold that they do not, that something American was denied. C.G. Road, Kahn's complex of buildings, and so many others are discrete, individual built projects, not policy and program advice, and not physical framework plans for an extended geographic region. Perhaps an answer lies therein: in Ahmedabad, we, no less than Kahn, were invited by local people to design a specific project, with specific clients, a reasonably specific program, achievable within a set time frame. The clients must have known whom they were bringing in and they were free to reject our designs. They chose to accept them. Presumably they are appropriate. Arguably, the clients for a plan for the Calcutta Metropolitan Area were many and difficult, if not impossible, to know (although this could be said for the Ahmedabad projects, too, though never to the same extent as in Calcutta); the program was vague and ever changing, and long range in timescale. Then, too, there is the matter of international economic pressures and power. The ability to undertake improvement projects in Calcutta was dependent to a considerable extent upon loans from international banking institutions. The loans might or might not be forthcoming, dependent upon their fitting in with a "plan." This was not so with the discrete Ahmedabad projects. In effect, in Calcutta, we, who were in good graces with the lenders, were saying, or implying, "Do a plan, preferably our kind of plan, maybe even *our* plan, or you might well not get the funding." There is something seriously wrong with that.

At the same time, all of this begs a question: do I want to contribute to physical globalization of urban physical environments? I would rather not. Kahn's

Ahmedabad project, I think, does not. Though unique, it does not shout, "Look at me!" It fits in. C.G. Road, because of the details of its design, notably its physical tightness, could never have been built in the U.S. Here we were saved by the place. One cannot get away from the problem, and the best answer I can come up with, even on discrete projects that are to be built in alien cultures, is: be very, very careful and be aware that you do not know very much about where you are working.

Some years ago, I was invited to Shanghai, along with Jaime Lerner, the Mayor of Curitiba, Brazil, a famous designer–planner. We were asked to make suggestions on a new city, Pudong, across the river from Shanghai. Given my predisposition about this kind of work, why did I go there? To see and perhaps to understand the problem; to find out if I wanted to be involved in its design; to see if my approach might be compatible with theirs; maybe simply ego or intellectual tourism. Lerner and I had the same approach: dense, low-rise development in a tight band along the river, preserving most of the rich farming land of the area for agriculture. This contrasted with ideas that we saw illustrated of spaced, very high-rise buildings that would eventually occupy all of the land. Clearly, our approach for Pudong was not wanted. Rather, Singapore and Hong Kong were the preferred models.

In relation to my "Why India?" conclusions, the China experience can be viewed in many ways. On the one hand, the hosts, the government clients, knew what they wanted. Our ideas were out of step and they politely said, "No thanks." Or it can be argued that the international city building models of New York, Tokyo, Singapore, and so on have overcome any notion of place-based city planning and urban design; that local people either aren't terribly interested in plan ideas that come from their own cultures and geography, except in details; or that physical plans are unimportant and that local people can and will adapt to whatever is built – the newer, shinier, and bigger, the better. And who are we to tell them that their plans should come out of their own historic contexts, let alone think we could know what those contexts are?

After my work experiences, and watching the nature of the developing world notwithstanding, I remain skeptical about abstract urban plans and working in places and among cultural environments about which I know little. The further I am away from home, the more cautious I get. Working in San Francisco, it took years to understand the environmental ethic of the city and the Bay Area – that it was grounded in climate, the Central Valley and the Sierra. How could a Midwesterner know, on a quick visit, of these matters, or truly understand appropriate urban responses to the never-ending cornfields of Nebraska? Perhaps I could rationalize an appropriate street design, but a whole plan for a metropolitan urban structure, for the Calcutta metropolitan region? If I get invited to India or another country these days, it is not because of expertise in such environments. Rather, it is because I have a particular set of understood skills – say, street design – that can be used to address a particular problem or set of problems. There is no such thing as an expert in the planning of developing countries. I suspect there is really no real expertise either, in knowing what is best for another people or culture.

Did I have to go to Calcutta to learn that? And did I have to drag my family with me? Perhaps I did, but one would hope that thoughtful people would understand that personal experience is not the only way to learn; that one ought to know that one doesn't know anything about some areas of the world and though learning about them might be a wonderful, enlightening, growing, and compassion-making experience, thinking that you can appropriately tell others how to grow and change and develop is a very questionable philosophy. One has the highest admiration for doctors and other health workers who go to places they knew little or nothing about for the sole purpose of human care. And, young or old, volunteers who are prepared to use their skills in the service of local people to combat poverty and want can do genuine service. I suspect that Rosser's bustee improvement program, at its most basic level, was in that category. We seem to do best in helping people and places when emergencies arise; in basic situations. Go, help, give money and supplies. Beware of the "shoulds" and particularly of attaching "And if you don't . . ." to the bargain.

The India experience was instructive in teaching me how to do my professional work in the U.S., particularly in coming to understand how little I could know about whatever past trends might portend. As Jaime Lerner says, "Trend is not destiny." Every creative act requires an element of leaping, to jump from what is known and has been to what might be. Deciding what is wanted or desired, and taking some leaps – reasonable ones, it is hoped; not off the cliff to rocks below – to achieve the desired state is exciting. Local people in Calcutta could have, probably would have, done that better without us.

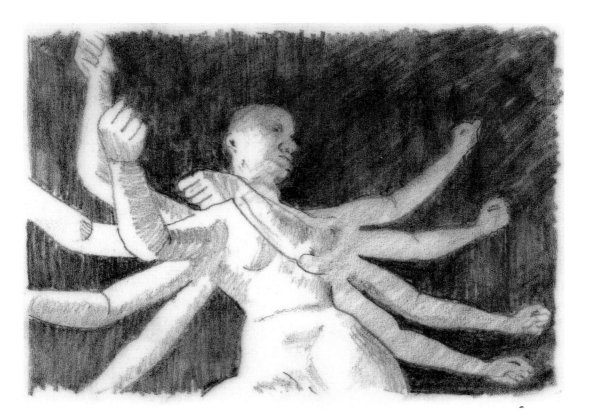

Clay Festival

In Piazza Navona

Part III

Learning
in Italy

View toward St. Peter's

Walls in Rome, near Vatican

Walls and Gates

There remain walls in and around many cities of Italy and much of Europe: city walls and gates. For three centuries, their original protective purposes thought to be long since past, walls were being torn down to be replaced by roads, parks, building projects, and, after World War II, superhighways. With an awakening of their significance in the continuity of community, the razing stopped and whatever was left of the walls, sometimes a little, sometimes much more, were kept and they remain, a part of the cityscape. The strange, ugly, modern Berlin Wall, an unnatural divider of people and community, was torn down as soon as there was a chance. Not so the older walls that remain in Italy. They are always grand. They are large, imposing, and usually of a warm, aged brick or stone. It is possible to imagine people at their turrets and their very existence makes you think about what life might have been like then – whenever "then" was – inside and outside of the walls or even on them. Now they are breaks in the inevitability of city development, places to breathe, a line to look along, toward the horizon or until the next turret, where the wall turns and goes out of sight. They provide nooks and crannies. The gates in the walls are usually narrow openings and they slow traffic, which is exactly what they were supposed to do. They were checkpoints. Today, even if there is no stopping or slowing down, the portal is eminently visible and one must think, I am coming into the city or I am going out. The experiences of the going and of the coming, the distinctions of the city and the country, or what used to be the country, are noted, marked. You are aware of yourself in that instant of walking or driving through the gates. Your time and place in relation to the whole community are marked. No traffic engineer would agree that the gates and walls are positive things, but that's all right, since they know only of uninterrupted movement and nothing of community.

Walls are okay, as long as there are open gateways through which to pass.

Monastery, Caprarola

Being Apart

At Caprarola, across a small ravine from the Palazzo Farnese and the sloping ridge on which the main street of the town is located, there is a church and attendant buildings, maybe a monastery or a school. There is a terrace at the top of a retaining wall that rises from the ravine and on that terrace and behind it sit the church and other buildings. There is a steep drop, over the retaining wall of the terrace and from one of the buildings, to the ravine. The buildings facing the terrace form a welcoming semi-enclosed rectangular entry, a piazza that looks over the ravine toward the town. There were two cars parked on the terrace. The church complex is in easy sight of the city, yet it is strongly separated by the ravine. There are no visible walks directly between the two, across the ravine. If you want to go from the town to the church, you have to take the long way around, away from both city and church, and then double-back on a reasonably level path. It would not be an overly long walk, maybe 20 minutes.

That complex has the best of two possible worlds: it is so very close to the community, close enough to be a part of it, within sound and even sight of the town's comings and goings, while being at the same time apart, distant enough to be separate, distinct, solitary. How nice, I thought. Wouldn't I like to live in that situation. To be sure, the inviting nature of the terrace had something to do with it, a complex of buildings with its own semi-enclosed piazza, urban in its own right, looking across to a more urban small town, climbing the ridge of a hill, starting or ending in the Palazzo Farnese.

Then, still looking across the ravine, another set of thoughts demanded attention. Only a few can be so well situated, apart but not apart. And who shall they be? If that location is indeed privileged, and it is, wouldn't everyone like to have it? Or one like it? But if everyone did, if everyone were indeed able to be slightly apart from all the others, then there would be no one in Caprarola, no climbing central street lined with terraces and small stores, no small piazza at which to gather, almost certainly fewer stores because they would have to be further apart and not enough people – people to buy things – would pass any one of them. Men and women, being apart, might not know each other as well as now and it is doubtful that they would meet in large numbers on the one main street as they do now on Sunday mornings and every evening. Or maybe there would be one institution, say, a church or a school, or one family left in Caprarola, and it, too, would be slightly apart, like all the others.

It strikes me that the church, or monastery, or whatever it is, is really the story of the evolution of urban life in much of the United States. It is not only the rich, or the powerful, or the somehow special who have wanted to be apart yet somehow attached to an urban community; it has been most people. And in the United States, in large measure they have had the technical ability and the wealth to be apart. Where they have done that, exercised the option to be apart, the city has diminished, or has ceased to be.

Gianicolo Busts

I had never seen anyone stop in front of one of those busts that accompany Garibaldi, up there on his horse, in the Gianicolo. They surround him and they sit on their pedestals along the grand, sycamore-lined streets that lead to him: Luigi Bartolucci, Ugo Bassi, Gustavo Modena, Angelo Tittori, Tomasso Salvini, Mattia Montecchi, Riciotti, Bruno and Costante Garibaldi, Maurizio Quadrio, Achille Sachi, Quirico Filopanti, and maybe 50 or 60 more fighters for nationhood, freedom, and independence. There are busts, too, that line walks and roads in the Villa Borghese, above the Piazza del Popolo: national heroes, painters, musicians, scientists, aviators, poets, sculptors and architects, athletes. No one stopped in front of them, either, except for a second or two. At least I'd never seen anyone stop. Then, one Saturday morning, early, before the bus-loads of tourists arrived, a lady stopped in front of General Avezzana. She was slight, erect, well dressed, mostly in black, with an expensive-looking tailored coat, and she had with her a small terrier on a leash. She stood in front of the bust, looked at it two or three times, looked down and then back up into his face, crossed herself and walked away, in the direction of Porto San Pancrazio.

I had never seen anything like that happen. Those busts are wonderful. Slightly larger than life size, you have to look up at them, but not much. Each is on a pedestal. Some have flamboyant hats, others uniforms cut off abruptly at the breast; still others are unadorned, seemingly in Roman style. They line the streets or walks. They have a rhythm to them, as do the trees, but the busts are white, and they contrast with the greens and browns; white marble exclamation points against green, every 20 feet or so. These were real people. Very few have been toppled. Oh, sure, Rossini's nose, like some others, has been broken. But no one has fooled around with Verdi. Just being there ties you to a past, to whatever they were or represented, even if you don't recognize the names. They catch the light and are very much present, even though no one seems to look at them.

Gianicolo busts

Sitting among them I had often wondered whether they were remembered as individuals. Was there a special day when the city put flowers or wreaths at their pedestals? A national heroes' day, perhaps. Were their birthdays ever remembered? Was there anyone left to remember them? I was certain that no one paid the statues any special attention. And then, that one day, there was that moment with the lady.

I wondered who she was. A granddaughter or great-granddaughter? A grand-niece? I could imagine only family. I wished it had been a child of a lover or a long-lost friend, or something like that. Did she care if she was seen? Avezzana looked very stern. I went back the next day and every day for more than a week at the same time as I had seen her. She never returned. I never saw her again.

But that lady was an inspiration to me and my friends. Now, on most Sunday mornings, we meet in front of one of those busts, between 11.30 and noon, when there are a lot of people strolling, before lunch. We always go to one of the statues near where there are likely to be people. We pay homage to one of them. We give grand memorial speeches. We try to do it near his birthday. We bring flowers and wreaths. People come to see what is going on; then they gather round and listen, respectfully. Sometimes one of the women dresses up in black and wears a veil and stands next to one of us. I always wear a black armband and black felt hat. I put my arms around her. She cries, sobbing quietly, visibly shaking. Once or twice a year, when we can afford it, we hire a uniformed band – black and red trim, and white leather belts and gold buttons – and it plays rousing music. On those days, we go to two or three different busts, a bit distant from each other, and pay homage all over again, making the most of our money. Sometimes one of us, dressed differently, interrupts a speech to let everyone know that our hero was not a hero at all but a fascist bastard, or a wife beater who left untold illegitimate children, or a communist pig, or lots of other things, and that we must therefore be fascist pigs, too. Sometimes a bastard great-grandchild, who just happens to be passing, denounces us. On some days there are fights and torn banners. Then we go for lunch and think about next week.

San Francisco should have a street lined with busts. They could be in Golden Gate Park, but a street would be better. Market Street! Market Street should have busts, about every 30 feet, on both sides, facing toward the sidewalks, from the Ferry Building to City Hall. That would be terrific! They would be in white marble and about seven feet high. On one side of the street there would be mayors and official heroes of the city. There could be a special commission to decide on the heroes. It might get very political, but that would be all right: over the years, it would even out as to who would be worthy of a bust. The city would pay for the busts of some of the heroes, certainly for the mayors, but maybe it wouldn't have the money, at least not all at once, for all the heroes. It might take a while. The other side of the street would be for anyone. If I wanted to have a bust of myself, I could have one, as long as I paid for both it and one of the official city heroes on the other side. That way the whole idea wouldn't cost the city very much. I'd do it. I'd love to have the chance to have a statue of myself on Market Street. Walter Shorenstein could have a statue too, if he wanted one. He could pay for ex-Mayor (now Senator) Feinstein's bust and for Willie Mays'. If I had enough money I'd buy one for my mother. She never lived in San Francisco, but without a bust I think she'll be forgotten, and I don't want that. And I'd get one of my father. And, if I had enough money, I'd get one of Ugo Bassi, not because I knew him or was related to him or anything like that, but because of the name: Ugo Bassi is a terrific name and there should be a bust of Ugo Bassi in every city. And there should be one of Etore and one of Massimo. Fabulous names, famous names, worthy names.

After all the years of trying to make Market Street a great street and after all the money spent trying to do that, the busts might just do the trick. All those statues marching up Market Street – it's the kind of idea that a national government should do, in Washington: line streets with heroes and presidents. People don't think like that any more, though, least of all in Washington. They think, there, in small ways, of national security and centralized power and big business, not big ideas, which is all the more reason for San Francisco to do it, alone, as a celebration of history and future and belonging to the community. In no time other cities would take the idea and do it better, or not as well. There is enough space, on all the streets of San Francisco, to have busts of every person who ever was or ever will be a citizen.

In the meantime, I noticed that there is one pedestal in the Gianicolo with no bust adorning it. So, at this very moment, my good friend Lorenzo Bruno is sculpting one of me, in a Roman fashion. When he has finished we will, one night, place the bust on the pedestal. I wonder if anyone will pay attention. Maybe, one Sunday, my friends will hold a celebration in front of it.

Via Costa Masciarelli

A Question of Values[1]

Cities change; their streets, their buildings, and of course their people. The physical changes are not always because of growth; sometimes the driving force is economic decline, which can be slow, so the changes are slow. But there are also the abrupt, often catastrophic changes caused by hurricanes, tsunamis, landslides, and earthquakes. The 2009 earthquake in L'Aquila, Italy, was such an event. Aside from the loss of life and great social and economic disruption to the community, the earthquake devastated beloved and priceless historic buildings and artifacts, and closed the downtown area as well as immediately surrounding areas to entry, habitation, and commerce. Some major historic buildings are gone, collapsed or damaged beyond repair. For others, the waiting game has started: what can or should be done to buildings, large and small, and when, and at what cost? And what of the city's infrastructure? All this in a community, like so many in Italy, whose people know and value the fabric of the built public environment, as well as the private, and was caring for that environment through many day-to-day improvements.

In 2003, on a walk with friends who live in the region, Elizabeth and I found ourselves on a newly remade street. The design details of the street, the quality of the materials used, and the fine workmanship caught our attention more than even the modest but compellingly simple historic residences that lined it. Neither we nor anyone else, I imagine, was thinking of an earthquake then.

We were walking on the Via Costa Masciarelli on a Sunday afternoon in early October, at about 6.30. The pavement was wet from day-long intermittent rain. There was still plenty of light. Via Costa Masciarelli leads down from and runs perpendicular to L'Aquila's main street, Corso Vittorio Emanuele, and central piazza toward a city gateway entrance that soon comes into sight after a

Via Costa Masciarelli

modest turn. Our purpose was nothing more than an early-evening stroll with friends.

L'Aquila is a city of about 100,000 people, in the Abruzzi, north and east of Rome, about one and a half hours by bus, up in the Apennines. It is an administrative center without significant industry, a bit too far to attract commuters to Rome, too close yet off the beaten track to attract tourists in large numbers: a provincial city. Say to friends that you have spent the weekend in L'Aquila and they are likely to ask you where it is. But the air is clear, there is skiing nearby during the winter, and the old, elegant castle is well worth seeing, as is a chapel in Santa Bernardino, with quite wonderful glazed terracottas by one of the della Robbia clan. There is (or was) a city orchestra, a city theater, a central piazza and many smaller ones, and good places to eat. This is Italy, after all.

After a first long, enthralling look down Via Costa Masciarelli to the recently restored, buff-colored city gateway, our attention focused on the sloping pavement of the street itself, divided into five lineal bands: two bands of sloping steps, 1.5 meters (5.9 feet) wide and 1 meter (3.28 feet) long; these bounded by three sloping surfaces, one along each row of buildings that define the street edge, and one in the center, between the two sets of steps. This central paved way is more for drainage than for walking. This is a street for people on foot, not for automobiles or other vehicles. Our close attention had nothing to do with autos, or the lack thereof, but with the slope, even of the steps, and of the wet stone paving, suggesting the possibility of a slippery downhill surface. Walking downhill on wet steps is often cause for a degree of care, it seems, if for no other reason than the steps are further away from one's eyes than when walking uphill. So we paid attention to our steps and to the stone paving, so clean, actually off-white, stone square insets, and concluded that the whole street had been recently rebuilt. For each of the walking paths, there is a sloping surface made of small white stone squares leading to a step, also of stone, that drops down to the next sloping surface. Each of the three unstepped surfaces, the two next to the buildings and the one for drainage between the walking paths, is made of the same white insets. The grout or cement between each stone is a light tan sand color. The actual risers on the sloping steps are of a buff-colored stone.

To someone accustomed to walking on concrete sidewalks in modern cities or even on the black stone cobbles of central Rome, the paving of Via Costa Masciarelli is a very attractive and well-executed walking surface. It is also new and looks to be expensive. The design quality, the newness, and the assumed cost prompted an initial question, from which others followed. Why did they do it this way? Weren't there less costly, more economical ways to rebuild the street? Is this a wealthy city, more so than we had been led to believe? Why this particular street? Is there community power here? Was it done for tourists? (Doubtful, as L'Aquila is not noted as a major tourist center.) Were alternatives considered? Assuming there were adequate funds for the project (it has been built, after all), what if there had been less money available? Maybe this is just the way they do things in L'Aquila, and, by extension, the way things are done in other Italian cities, small and large alike. The black stone paving blocks of central Rome seem to be a constant; and we are advised that some, maybe all, now come from China. In the end, that is our hypothesis: it's just the way they do it. Italians knew there were other, less expensive ways of paving a street, even one of importance, but those ways would not be appropriate; not "right." That is the answer we'd like to be closest to the truth: it's a question of values; not so much, or very much at all, of monetary or economic values but of historical, deeply held, cultural values. Even as we think this, we imagine economist colleagues shaking their heads in disagreement, if not disbelief, insisting that costs and benefits and available fiscal resources had everything to do with the rebuilding of the street and that design aesthetics were made to fit economic reality. The whole endeavor may be called into question. Did the street designers or those who approved the project not give a whit for the whole city or all of its streets, to say nothing of important uses, other than street paving, to which the funds could more usefully be put: costs and benefits. Were not fine but less expensive designs possible? Why wasn't Via Costa Masciarelli paved with asphalt and precast concrete steps? Or why not use large, handsome, precast pavers, attractively set, as we observed on a recently executed major public way in Massa Maritima: more expensive than asphalt but a fraction of what we were seeing in L'Aquila.

These reactions – questions, really – crowded through our heads as we enjoyed the walk down to Via Fortebraccio, where we turned left, rising toward S. Bernardino. This street, too, is well paved. We would like to find out why the Via Costa Masciarelli was refinished the way it was. Perhaps it would be possible to return, if only for a day or two, to find some answers.

L'Aquila is a Roman city. A clue to the historic importance of Via Costa Masciarelli is its focus at one end on an old city gate; not too many streets do that. Less obvious, on the ground, is that, together with Via Paradiso (or Via Cimino, or Strada di S. Domenico), it forms a major east–west spine of the city, meeting the more important Corso Vittorio Emanuele at the city's main piazza, Piazza Maggiore (or Piazza Grande, Piazza del Duomo, or Piazza del Mercato, depending on which plan or map one is consulting). The city was destroyed in the middle of the 13th century. It was rebuilt, at some speed, starting in the early 14th century. As was so often the case in the building of Italian cities, L'Aquila's builders quarried stone from the "old" Roman city to build the new one, widening its streets. And, indeed, the more recent design and reconstruction of Via Costa Masciarelli did focus on making the street as much as possible as it had been in earlier times. To put it simply, as it was a very important, historic city street, the aim was to rebuild it the way it had been.

It helps, of course, to know what the street and city had been, to know its importance, and to have a model to shoot for. There are historical references for L'Aquila – if not precise details of street paving, certainly records of the historic growth of the city and even of typical building conventions, as expressed in detailed drawings. From these, and from discussions with L'Aquila's architect–town planner, we come to understand that the redesigners of Via Costa Masciarelli knew full well that the reconstruction would be expensive, but also that the state (through the Superintendenza Archeologicia), rather than the city, would pay in order to do the street "right."

We wonder what would have happened if the state hadn't provided the money. The answer is uncompromising: "They find the money." But if that really had not been possible, would the street not have been fixed? Or would the city have found private individuals willing to pay for the design in exchange for glory: a remnant of the days of great art connected to the Church and grand patrons? We are shown a newly repaved piazza outside the architect's office, with its lower quality stone, and are reminded that it is "not as good." In reality, that is the answer: without adequate funds, even on Via Costa Masciarelli, the work might well have been done, only less expensively, and perhaps less well. But, importantly, there would be community knowledge and memory that the street repaving was not of the quality it should be.

In our local enquiries, we sensed a reluctance to deal with the question of what if there had not been enough money. Finally, after some thought, we were advised that the repaving of Via Costa Masciarelli was a matter of community identity that remains important in L'Aquila. If the money wasn't there, then they would either not do it at all or would do it less well, in the knowledge that the work would have to be done again at a later date in order for it to be "right."

In our discussions, it was difficult to get to the question of economic value in this matter of public works. Eventually, we were advised that economic value is relative. In the market of public works, we were told, the value of identity is held to be stable (even if we know this to be untrue). Economic value, on the other hand, changes. In comparison, the *identity* value is always superior. At least, that's the theory. It is a short way of saying that cultural values, remembering and honoring the past, the historic fabric, are important in L'Aquila, particularly in the public realm. A public space in the historic center required more than utilitarian treatment and attention, a deference to people on foot, no blind use of standardized materials and details, but knowledge of or reference to the past.

At the time of writing (summer 2010), Via Costa Masciarelli, as well as the historic downtown, is in L'Aquila's "Red Zone," which means that no one is allowed there, not even if their houses are on the street. Some buildings in the central area collapsed; others were severely damaged. The entire area, in the words of a friend, "is a mess." Stores are now to be found in surrounding shopping centers. New houses have been built, quickly, on the outskirts of town. They are of a quality, we are told, that may not last. L'Aquila, we feel certain, *will* last. But as what? If one takes a long view, say at least 50 and maybe 100 years, one might reasonably assume that there will be a busy town center that replaces the old one. It may even be of a similar scale. The history of Italian urbanism is long; and people, including those with access to historic records, remember what once was and honor it, even without always feeling the need to replicate the past. We suspect that there will be a pedestrian-scaled public realm. As for the wonderful central castle, as contemporary in design as it is old, what of it? We can only hope.

And what of Via Costa Masciarelli? The street is still there and so are the houses, in various conditions. The street, we think, will remain. And its elegant, historic surfacing? Even if it is in ruin – and we do not know that it is – the city has those records of what it has been, and will know its value.

Note

1   This essay is an updated version of "Via Costa Masciarelli," *Places*, 16(3) (2004), pp. 32–35.

Old City Gate, L'Aquila

Part IV

City People

Fragments

Traffic Cop

At the entrance to the grounds of the Imperial Palace, in Tokyo, well past the outer moat, at the one main street that passes north to south through this area, but before the inner moat that is the limit of penetration permitted for the everyday person, there is a traffic cop whose job it is to make sure that everyone, especially pedestrians, obeys the traffic rules. Well, he's sort of a cop; he wears an orange vest that says "STAFF" and he has a bullhorn that he uses. His mien is stern and he seems very serious. He makes sure that people obey the rules. He stops cyclists crossing against the light when it's the pedestrians' turn. He makes sure that pedestrians walk exactly where they are supposed to walk, and even if you are 300 or so feet away and jay-walk, he spots you, turns on the bullhorn, and orders you back to where you came from. Having seen him do that to one poor soul, I would not have dared to walk at the wrong time or place. He demands that a passing roller-blader get off the street and onto one of the walks. Young people laugh at him, but they still obey the rules. A reason for the laughter, I think, is that there are no cars and precious few cyclists or pedestrians. It's Sunday and cars aren't permitted on that street on a Sunday. So, what is he directing? It must be a matter of principle: do things right, always. Obey the law. He's an older man. I wonder if he's there during the week. Do the people laugh, and obey, because they understand that for that man this is an important job and it won't kill them to pay attention to him? On my way back from a failed watercolor at the inner moat of the palace the pedestrian light is changing as I cross and I rush to the median island hoping he won't spot me. He does. Our eyes meet, we both smile, and grunt. When he goes home at the end of the day, does he have the satisfaction of a job well done? He should!

Excellent!

There is a young, pleasant man who works at the tennis and swim club I frequent, and he is much taken with the word "excellent." On every occasion that we have met, he has said "excellent." He says it with gusto, joy, and a smile.

Ernesto does a lot of things at the club, although they have changed over the years. He started as one of the employees who picks up soiled towels and delivers clean ones to various places in the club. Probably he had something to do with their washing, drying, and folding as well. Now, he works around the grounds, is responsible for keeping the swimming-pool water clear, attends to the courts, and seems to be in charge of some people, including his successors as towel distributors. He is always in a bit of a hurry, and our conversations are limited to simple greetings.

"Hello. How are you?"

"Fine. How are you?"

"EXCELLENT!"

Ernesto is from a Latin American country. The very brief "hello" and "how are you?" reveal our respective origins. English is not his native language. Perhaps he learned it as an adult and in the process became enthralled with "excellent": its sound, its quick constriction at the back and the top of the mouth, followed by widening the mouth and a quick flex of the cheek muscles to say the "ell," and the push of the tongue against the upper teeth at the staccato ending, like a bullet. "EKS . . . ELL . . . ENT!" I think he just loves to say it.

Ernesto and I come across each other and he never fails to say, "Hello. How are you?"

I always answer, "Fine. How are you?" And he says, with a smile and emphasis, "EXCELLENT!" There's an emphasis on the "ex." Ernesto never stops at "Hello." He always asks about my well-being. And it is clear to me that he expects a similar question in return. For sure, I could reply, simply, "Fine," or "Good," or "So-so," or even "Average," or "Not-so-hot," and let it go at that, without enquiring as to Ernesto's state. Early on, that would have been unthinkable. Later, it would have been rude, at best. Now, it would be nasty. But I still think about it. I spot Ernesto coming my way and anticipate the routine, half wondering how to break it, thinking bad thoughts that would elicit no "Excellent!" and half dying to hear it.

"Fine. How are you?"

"Excellent!"

Some years ago, at the tollbooths of the San Francisco–Oakland Bay Bridge, there was a toll-taker who would take my money and say, "How are you?" I'd reply, "Fine," and follow with, "How are you?" To which he'd say, "I'm blessed!" He was blessed. There was something of a smile to his face, an almost smile, the smile of the blessed. The rapid give-and-take of my payment, even if he had to make change for a ten or a twenty, allowed no more discussion than that, which was okay with me. I sensed he would have liked a word or two more. His job must be one of the worst in the world, hours on end of taking money and giving change from a cramped, cold or hot, booth; nothing more. How do people deal with that job? By being blessed. My path would cross his lane and work shift maybe once every two or three weeks and the routine was always the same, ending with "I'm blessed!"

It began to bug me that God or some other deity had snuck into our conversations. I really didn't want to hear about him being blessed. One day he asked me how I was and I said, "Fine," let it drop at that, then drove on. He looked a bit surprised. The next time we met I did the same thing, and this time he appeared sour, maybe even angry. There then followed a long period during which I didn't come across him at a tollbooth, a year and a half, perhaps two. On occasion, I would wonder what had happened to him.

Of late, maybe for the last six months, he's been back. He takes the money, gives the change. There is no conversation – no "hello," no "thank-you" – which isn't so different than other toll-takers. But he looks grim, even angry, during the transaction. There is no spark and certainly no recognition of me. Our eyes do not meet. Or do they? It is only now that I wonder, for the first time, if my calculated non-response to his "How are you?" was in part responsible for his change. That seems far-fetched. I reject it. At the same time, I envision stopping at his booth one day and asking, "How are you?" and him replying, "Go fuck yourself." That might be the starting point for a reconciliation. But I don't want to start hearing about him being blessed again. Of course, I could always say, "Me too!"

One wants to be careful what one says, but I must admit that there's a piece of me that wants to say "Excellent!" the next time Ernesto asks how I am. The trouble is that I could never say it as well as he does, and I would risk never hearing him say it again.

Immigrants

Mr. Yong Yu and his wife own and run the coffee shop on the corner of Queen Street. We have become acquaintances. He likes to talk with me, it seems. Shortly after I started to go there for afternoon coffee, and shortly after he saw me one Sunday sitting on a bench outside the children's painting and craft store, next to his coffee shop, painting a watercolor of the buildings across the street, he started talking to me whenever I came in. His wife's name is unknown to me, and I am not sure if it would be proper to ask what it is.

One afternoon, as I was leaving, Mr. Yu asked if I was a painter and I said that I was, which is a half-truth, at best. But I told him as well that I taught school and that I came from San Francisco. That was about the extent of our first discussion.

How to decide to go to one coffee shop over another on Queen Street, in the Beaches, in Toronto? There are so many of them. One has to see the shop, know that it exists, to start. Toward the end of the Beaches, shortly before the streetcar turns around for the nine-mile trip back through downtown and beyond, the intensive commercial uses begin to peter out and there are far fewer people on the street than further west. There are no Starbucks, or Second Cups, or Coffee Times here. The stores are mostly local food shops. But there is a local movie house that's hanging on, as well as an ice-cream store, a couple of restaurants, two bars, two coffee shops, and a collection of food stores and hardware stores. So there are choices. One of the coffee shops is on the north side of the street and gets the sun, but a friend has spoken poorly of it. Quigley's, at the corner, seems more of a drinking and eating establishment, with a good-sized area of outdoor tables and lights between the building and the side-street that intersects Queen Street. It seems to be a local hang-out. Certainly one could get a cup of coffee in there. Directly across the street, on the south side, the

Best Coffee House is very modest, and a bit dark because the sun doesn't shine on it. It has the slightest look of an English tearoom. This is Mr. and Mrs. Yu's place.

Mr. Yu seems to want to talk whenever I am there, but he does not insinuate himself. He doesn't rush into conversation. One day, while I am on one of the higher stools by the front window, across from the counter, he sees that I am not reading and he talks about painting. He cannot do it, he says, and he does not know much about it, but he likes paintings. They touch him, he says, and he puts one hand up, toward his chest. On another day he asks me to explain the difference between oil painting and watercolor painting. He tells me of famous paintings in Korea that are done with pulverized black inks mixed, he thinks, with water.

Mr. and Mrs. Yu are in their shop every day. It opens at seven in the morning and closes at six. One Sunday Mr. Yu acknowledges that their days are long and hard. It takes them about 45 minutes each way to drive to and from their home in the northern part of the city. I suggest that it is hard to keep working seven days a week and that perhaps they should take some time off. He says there is not enough business and that it is important to be open every day. His customers expect it and he fears losing them.

Another day Mr. Yu speaks more of his life. He comes from Korea and has been in Canada for 15 months. His first choice was the U.S. but, he says, it is very expensive and harder to get into. In Korea, he worked for a food company and had been to the States a number of times, both to buy materials and to sell products. He has a brother in New York and a sister in Chicago, so he would rather have gone to the U.S. He is 48 years old. He spent some time looking for the right business opportunity before opening the coffee shop.

The Yus have a son who is 19 and studying to get into college, which Mr. Yu thinks will be next year. At Mr. Yu's urging the son will pursue computer sciences. Then, perhaps, they will move closer to the coffee shop. But a move would be disruptive now. The success of the coffee shop may have something to do with whether a move is possible, but Mr. Yu does not say this.

There is always music in the shop. Mostly it is Nat King Cole, but sometimes operatic arias. A young girl helps out on Saturdays and Sundays. Mr. Yu says that they also have help in the mornings, but that the young men or boys who he has hired don't work hard and don't pay enough attention to the customers. They seem more interested in reading the paper and respond with grunts to people's orders. He generalizes about the young people and their non-work habits. Life for him and Mrs. Yu in Canada is very difficult. They must work very hard. He likes to play golf but has not done so since coming to Canada.

One day Mr. Yu is out when I enter the shop. He was there earlier. In greeting Mrs. Yu, I ask how she is and she says, "Not too good!" Does she have a cold? "No, that isn't it. Sometimes my language is not so good and some customers become angry because I don't understand and sometimes I make the wrong thing." Perhaps she could smile (as she always does) and tell them that she is sorry, but her language is not so good, and could they please speak more slowly? She says that sometimes she does that but that it doesn't always work. Most customers, she says, are nice and understanding, but some are not. "Actually," she says, "when my husband made the decision to move to Canada, I did not like it. Even now I feel that way." She says it is hard to make friends.

The next day Mrs. Yu is not in the shop. Mr. Yu is behind the counter with a young lady who is helping him. They say that Mrs. Yu was tired and decided to stay home that day. Later, Mr. Yu explains that he has rearranged the outside tables in a manner that will allow him to park his car, at least for the winter months that are coming. We talk about the possibility of a bit more light inside the shop's entry and windows, to make up for the darkness of this side of the street, and thereby to make it more visible. Mr. Yu says that he will not take a day off at least until the holidays in December. He says that business is all right. After a pause, he admits that it could be better.

Three years have passed. Queen Street, out toward the Beaches, looks much the same, but there have been changes in detail. Across from Kew Gardens, on a property that had a fire, there is a new building: two stores at ground level plus three floors of housing that step back from the front. The scale of the stores is narrow, as before, but the building is taller by two floors. The small pharmacy at a corner has been replaced by a store that sells art objects, not too expensive. The small movie house has a new marquee, and the corner superette is newly painted, with improvements to the inside as well. The small greengrocer's has closed. Inside Best Coffee House, in late morning, I am the only customer. Two women are at the front, near the doorway, talking. In time, I ask them about Mr. and Mrs. Yu. This is no longer their store. Mr. Yu "is in insurance," and Mrs. Yu, I am told, is "in a laundry store."

Practicing

Lorenzo and I went for a drive on Sunday. We went to see the Palazzo Farnese at Caprarola, and then we toured the area: Lago di Vico and some of the small towns that we'd passed on other trips; towns that beckoned from a short distance off the main road; towns whose tight, hillside shapes always invited; towns like hundreds of others yet that seemed individually special; towns that I always wanted to see, but never had. We stopped at Ronciglione and Sutri and Capranica.

We reached Capranica late in the afternoon. The entrance is just off a sharp bend in the road, and it's a true entrance. There's a gate, a portal, and a glimpse of the main street, rising into the town. You knew when you were entering and leaving, or passing, Capranica. Just outside the gateway, and what is left of the town walls, there is a bosque of trees in a level piazza area that looks over the countryside, a belvedere. There are retaining walls. Whenever we had passed Capranica before, there were at least a few men standing or sitting in that piazza, in sun or shade, as might suit them. They were older men. They saw you go by. They were there when we drove into the town, through the gate, on Sunday afternoon; more than we had seen when passing on other days.

We parked on the main street and spent about an hour walking up and down. An event of some sort had just concluded at the first church we passed. There was a knot of people, beginning to disperse. Standing in the small piazza, in front of the church, and off the main street, a small amount of very light soot or ash floated down. As we walked we concocted a story about soot as the ultimate compound for polishing copper etching plates and the man from this very town who made the discovery, but died in ignominy after burning down the community forest one day while trying to produce a large amount of soot and fine, fine ash to sell all over the world. He said he wanted only to bring prosperity and fame to his city. The town condemned him to live in the ashes of the forest he had burned and later he was stoned to death when it was discovered he had been approaching young girls, trying to market his soot as the talcum that could make their skins the smoothest and silkiest in all of Italy. Actually, Lorenzo told me, Francesco Petrarch had come from this town and had brought it some measure of fame.

The streets – the one main street, really – were not crowded but there were people strolling, mostly in pairs, some families. A lot of people stopped and talked, or greeted each other in passing. After a while, we were aware of seeing the same people walking in opposite directions. It was the time of day when people come out, walk, talk, see again the people they might have seen earlier, before lunch or the day before.

The most compelling thing about Capranica, on Sunday, was the entrance piazza and the older men standing and sitting. There were men like that at one place or another in every Italian city or town. We decided to visit them and to practice being older. So we walked back through the gateway to where the old men were. We watched them to see what we would have to do if we wanted to be like them. If you want to be older, in the Italian fashion, it's best to wear a pair of pants and a jacket that don't quite match. The jacket or the pants are from different suits. It's best if they are a bit too large. You wear a tie. Hats and caps are all right, but not required. Shoes are black, middle-weight or on the heavy side; no high style here. Some of the men stand and others sit.

After watching them for a short while we decided to join the sitters on one of the low retaining walls. Sitting the way those older guys do takes a little practice. They don't sit back, not one of them. They lean forward, not using much of their asses. We leaned forward, too. The sitters don't talk to each other very much. Mostly they just sit and look forward. Lorenzo and I stopped talking. I'm sure they watch the people passing, but they don't move their heads very much. The standers are more animated. They stand in tight circles. There are one or two men around the edges. The ones at the edges don't talk, but they nod and smile a lot. There are no women with the men outside the gate. But women pass, usually in pairs; two women walking, talking to each other. The women and the men barely notice each other. One passing woman says hello to one of the men. He and his companions return the greeting, with formality and a respectful bow of heads.

As evening approached, there seemed to be fewer men. Singly or as couples, they left. It was time for us to go, too. I don't think that it would take a lot of practice to become old in Capranica, or Palombara Sabina, or most of the big and small cities I had seen in Italy. I think you just fall into it, with grace.

On Thursday, we visited Palombara Sabina, also small and hilly, with an ancient castle being restored. We had first been to S. Angelo Romano, so we did not arrive until 4.00 in the afternoon. Lorenzo went off to paint and I decided to sit in the park – another belvedere, really – that looks over the valley to the hills beyond. Again there were ten older men both sitting and standing, some in the sunshine, others under the trees. I drew them, while observing and maybe practicing for the inevitable.

Part V

Breaking and Making Community

Cleveland and the Unmaking of City

My family's progression of housing locations followed a pattern typical of that which was the undoing of Cleveland as a city: from an apartment above stores at East 105th Street and Greenlawn Avenue to a rented single family house not far away on Amor Avenue, to another apartment, this time without stores, just a bit further out, on Lakeview Road, and then up to Bellfield Road in Cleveland Heights, the first ring of eastern suburbs. My brother and his family would continue the outward moves: first to a modest house in South Euclid, the third suburb east, and then to a more substantial home, a bit further out, to raise three daughters who, in turn, moved still further out to places like the outskirts of Akron and Columbus. An aunt, in the meantime, moved from that East 105th Street apartment to Cleveland Heights, and then to a nice town, Stow, now considered a suburb. In my time I would move out altogether, with several stops before settling in San Francisco.

In 2006, I visited my brother in South Euclid, my first time there in almost ten years. During a stay of four days we headed west, toward what was once downtown, only one time, a trip to satisfy my curiosity about what had been done in all that space between the Severence Hall and the Cleveland Museum of Art complex, just past East 106th Street, and the central Terminal Tower, a distance of over 100 blocks, an area devastated during the racial tensions of the 1960s. Precious little! Sure, the Cleveland Clinic had spread in every direction between Carnegie and Euclid avenues, but it is basically an inward-oriented fortress. Cleveland State University, closer to the old downtown, spreads as well. Mostly, there is a wasteland over those 100 or so blocks. But, more importantly, in my four days that one trip was the only one we took that was westward, toward the old city. All the others were outward. Every destination was outward. On my last day in Cleveland we went east, to visit my brother's get-away-and-relax condominium apartment on Lake Erie, near Ashtabula, then southward to one of his daughter's houses, and then to a restaurant for a family meal, near Akron. In a long day out, about 16 hours, at least six and probably eight of those hours were spent in a car.

On the previous day an old friend toured me around as we remembered old times. All that travel, too, was outward; his choice, not mine. Traveling the rolling landscape, to see new housing developments, he confirmed that the city's population was now about 450,000, less than one-half of its high point. But, he said, it was stable, if not growing. So why were there all these new housing subdivisions that he was driving me around? Who was filling the new, undistinguished, large housing on large lots? Mostly people from the suburbs closer to Cleveland. People keep moving outward, just like when I was a kid, but now not from the city; from the suburbs. Indeed, my brother advised me that his quite wonderful house – brick, large rooms, much woodwork, slate roof, leaded glass casement windows, beamed ceilings, a double-size lot with large, mature trees, a gently undulating street with other fine homes – was worth maybe $200,000, plus or minus, less than what it once would have brought. In the Bay Area it would easily bring $1,500,000. *Lots* like his sell for over $900,000 in San Francisco. His area is less desirable than it once was; too far in. People of more modest means, often of color, are moving into their neighborhood; and maybe that's wonderful. Racism was not a reason for him and his wife to move; advancing age was. Their move was outward. None of this outward ooze is new. It has been going on at least since our first move from the city to Cleveland Heights, almost 70 years ago. It takes a long time to drain a city; 70 years and still not done.

People come to cities and stay in them for opportunities that will make their lives better, mostly to work and gain an income. When there is no work they may invent new things to do that bring sustenance, or they may leave, for places with greater promise. Cleveland was heavy industry: steel, shipping, heavy machinery, tools, trucks, ball bearings, clothing, turret lathes; big stuff, small stuff. And there were opportunities for sales and services that come with the making and selling of things and, with working people, stores of all kinds, and doctors, insurance offices, and churches. In time, if what is produced is no longer relevant to society, or is available at less cost from elsewhere, then factories and businesses may close and people may move elsewhere, and others may stop coming. That seems to be what happened in and around Cleveland, starting in the 1960s. Movement outward from the center started earlier, but at least in part it was associated with population change. The same could be said for Detroit and St. Louis and Kansas City, of course. In Cleveland, Warner and Swazey Company, makers of turret lathes, was closing, or soon would be; and Thompson Products, with their airplane engine parts, was leaving; and others as well. Republic Steel would last longer.

The demise of Cleveland as a vibrant, active city might be associated with the loss of its economic base, the same as can be said about so many of the "rust belt" cities. Failing cities, of course, are nothing new. Changing geography or disappearing resources were often causes. And so, Brugge, once *a*, if not *the*, world wool capital, watched its waterways clog with silt, and its economy clog with the sand. Montpellier was once a major cosmopolitan port city until the Mediterranean shoreline moved a bit south – not far, but far enough. The water ran out at Shah Jahan's Fatipur Sikri, and though he had his promised son there, he was forced to move the capital back to Agra. Brugge and Montpellier have long since "come back" and are thriving, if smallish, cities. Economic activities different from what made them major centers in the first place, over time, have been found or developed, and those cities seem to be doing very well. Not so Fatipur Sikri, a city of royal whim and not much else.

There are many examples of small cities that have revived. It is somewhat harder to enumerate major cities whose economic base ceased and which later came to thrive with new economic foundations. The point here, though, is that the Cleveland Metropolitan Area, despite its shrinking economic base and its stagnant (at best) population size, continues to grow physically, expanding its developed area ever outward, consuming what was once productive farmland. In doing so, the hole in the doughnut seems to become ever larger. Maybe it is really not a hole in the center: a better characterization might be an unurbanizing of the central city surrounded by a low-, low- density area.

In a sense, Cleveland – and the other Clevelands – seems to fit the model predicted by the academic regional economists of the 1960s and 1970s, who talked about spread urban development as if it were some kind of natural law, with associated declines in densities (and height) in city centers, a kind of "Broadacre City," all based on sophisticated models that earned Ph.D.s for soon-to-be academics. They may very well have been correct as applied to the Clevelands of the world. But they sure didn't explain San Francisco or many-centered Los Angeles, or what would soon be true of Vancouver. These economists seemed to have no use for the possibility of communities understanding their situations, deciding with foresight what future possibilities were and what they wanted to be, and then setting out courses of action to achieve desired ends; in short, planning. Trend, analyzed with sophistication, was everything. Would they even consider the possibility that trend is not destiny?

The trend in Cleveland, however, continues – outward, ever outward, sprawling development. The demise of Cleveland as a true urban place has been aided and abetted, in no small way, by local decisions that have pushed it along. Cleveland once had a wonderful public transportation system, of streetcars and buses that criss-crossed the city, with a weight of service that favored downtown and a focus at Public Square. As a kid I could get downtown by any of three streetcar lines, to high school by either of two, to my grandmother's via transfers at 105th Street. As a teenager, I could get to work at Chicago Pneumatic Tool Company, on St. Clair Avenue, via the Cedar or Fairmount Boulevard lines, a transfer at 79th Street to a bus, and then another transfer to the St. Clair streetcar that got me to work. The whole trip took less than an hour,

the toughest part being the walk down my street in the cold, dark, early mornings. The streetcars began to go in the late 1940s or early 1950s, victims of a
growing enthrallment with the automobile, ceding the centers of streets to
Detroit's faster, more agile products, and falling prey to General Motors' nasty
campaigns to replace them with buses. It wasn't inevitable. It didn't have to
happen. It sure didn't do anything good for downtown or the central city. It made
the fringes easier to reach. Local land economists, with their market predictions,
encouraged outward development. That was the future.

Voters of Cuyahoga County, in the early post-World War II years, with
urging from professionals, decided that a rapid transit line, east–west through
the city center, would serve transit better than all those streetcar and bus lines.
A single line was built. Trouble was that it followed old routes of the city's many
rail lines, the line of least resistance: the stops neatly avoided proximity to where
people lived or, with the exception of one downtown stop, where they might
want to go. Buses, from neighborhoods, came to the transit stops, and people
had to transfer to the rapid; not always easy when the tracks were well above
or below ground level, on a trestle or in a ravine, where the rail lines were
located. Do you know a lot of good housing areas situated next to old rail lines?
The one downtown station was at the Terminal Tower, the westernmost location
in the central area. What about access to the better department stores, further
east, and to the movie-house area, still further on, and the banking area at East
9th Street? Nothing! And the new transit system avoided Euclid Avenue and the
105th Street shopping area altogether. Bonds to build a downtown loop didn't
get issued for a period of six years, by which time their possibility had lapsed.
Voters again approved a bond issue, and again the project was scuttled.

Downtown Cleveland is today largely dead, not unlike downtown Kansas
City when I visited in 2005. Development in Cleveland continues outward. The
Rock and Roll Hall of Fame, down by the long-ignored and still largely inacces-
sible lake front, does not exactly a city make; nor is it likely to do so.

What of Cleveland's future? And the other Clevelands, what of them?

Doing nothing is certainly an option. Let the market decide; if spread city
is what the people want – and no city might be a better characterization – then
so be it. We can study the phenomena attendant to simultaneous metropolitan
spread and demographic–economic decline, and we can develop and apply
sophisticated formulas, but do not have thoughts or inclinations about changing
the natural order of things. Such public initiatives, some might call them planning,
never really work. Let matters take their course. In this view there is no such
thing as wasting land or natural resources, particularly in a land of plenty.
Pollution and waste are, in the grand scheme of things, momentary, to be
corrected in time (how much time?) by an unfettered free economy.

None of this may make any sense: polluted air, toxic land, desert where
once water flowed are not momentary phenomena and do not cure themselves
via the market, except perhaps in the longest time sense, when, with so much
having gone to hell, the market can start over, after centuries at best, eons more

likely. In what must be one of the most cynical observations of recent times – cynical if it weren't so everyday – Ben Bernanke, chair of the Federal Reserve, is reported to have said, in regards to the huge mortgage fiasco of 2007, "Market discipline has, in some cases, broken down, and the incentives to follow prudent lending procedures have, at times, eroded" (Paul Krugman in the *New York Times*, December 21, 2007). Yeah, like it doesn't happen every Tuesday and Thursday. Experience suggests that the free-marketers don't want intervention or controls unless their malpractices are found out and they are in financial trouble. *Then* they want help – for which read subsidies.

After the 1950s, government (federal, state, local) and development response to vast areas of urban deterioration has been something called re-development: government acquisition and assembly of properties, clearance, and redevelopment, presumably to respond to social needs. Often as not, the consequences have been less than lovely physically and more than a little unfortunate socially. How have Vancouverites managed to do large-land projects well, while American cities have in general done them so poorly? All of the Clevelands and Detroits can point to more distressing than positive project examples. It has much to do, one suspects, with very constrained general markets to start, with general anti-urbanism in much of the Midwest, and with an unwillingness and inability on the part of local planners and developers, very much including government officials, elected and appointed alike, to envision what good urbanism is; and even less willingness to hang tough with policies that could ensure real city building.

A somewhat radical response to the what-to-do question might start with the admonition to plant trees, then vegetables, and other agricultural products, and to do it for environmental, economic, and social reasons. One is aware of proposals like this for some of the once-developed urban wildernesses of cities like Detroit.

Trees and other plants are not generally thought of as urban. But, then, Cleveland and so many other cities are no longer urban places. Cleveland was once known as the "forest city," and maybe, just maybe, that's where its best future lies. Why leave all that once-developed land, now basically vacant or dotted with derelict or worse buildings alone, to stand waiting for some dream future, the newest Silicon Valley, to take its place? That's not likely to happen; and in any case this is the land of spread, at least for now. So why not plant and maintain trees, as economic and social ventures, undertakings that would be environmentally, socially, and spiritually healthy and uplifting as well? Informal woodsy plantings, formal rows and bosques, playful and somber, arrangements thus far undreamed of. Grow trees for their wood, for fiber, for food, as nurseries, as air filters, as maskers of what once was. Employment per tree, for planting, maintaining, harvesting, might not be high, or high paying, but there would be ways to earn a living that there are not presently. And food crops; urban farming. The amounts of agricultural land in Italian cities, even large ones like Bologna and Rome, are remarkable. Jaime Lerner, inveterate city-builder and sloganeer, once said of the fruit-tree plantings on Curitiba's public land that the people might have a right to a certain number of kilos of fruit from public orchards. But the growing of food – fruits, vegetables, even grain – on presently vacant land, much of it public land, in greenhouses as well as in non-toxic soil, can be thought of and developed as economic ventures (perhaps with a public start-up nudge on public land) as well as job sources.

People in low-income neighborhoods often rightfully complain of the dearth of local food outlets, including supermarkets, in their localities, and the high costs of getting to the closest one, to say nothing of the high prices. Imagine three greenhouses, side by side on some currently vacant property in Cleveland, growing a variety of cash crops: lettuce, tomatoes, squash, corn, cucumbers, potatoes, and on and on. Then imagine the front third of one of the greenhouses devoted to marketing the products. People would work at planting, growing, harvesting, selling; in other words, farming. They would be paid for their work. They might form cooperatives. The market for the produce need not be wholly local; with sufficiently high quality it could be regional or even national. And, by the way, what else is there to do with so much of this land? Wait? For what?

Some years ago, in St. Louis, I paid a ritual visit to what had once been the infamous Pruitt-Igoe public housing development, then long since cleared of its demolished buildings. In its place were a new school, one other structure, and much weed-covered rubble, fully 15 or 20 years after the demolition. I could not help thinking, Why leave that land sitting like that, so desolate, so demanding a remembrance of the previous nastiness? Why not cover the site with rows of trees. By the time of my visit they would already have been a developing urban forest, a place to visit for its own goodness. I don't know what has happened on that site since my last trip. Hopefully something fine. Whatever has happened, is it better than an urban forest–park?

Myths have it that there was a time in the U.S. when a squirrel, if it wished, could travel from the Atlantic to the Pacific without touching the ground. It could cover the distance via tree limbs. For sure, the trees–forest–agriculture idea is not an urban solution to vacant, derelict land and buildings in Cleveland or other such municipal corporate landscapes. It recognizes, though, that many Americans, particularly in the Midwest, just don't like cities; they prefer aloneness where they live and travel. Fine, at least until the ecological and socio-economic costs truly catch up with them, which will probably be sooner rather than later. But reality can be a long time coming, I've found. So, for now at least, do something useful – and by the way attractive – with all that's been left behind.

There is another attractive alternative to what has happened to Cleveland and elsewhere: take the once-developed land that has come into city hands via tax delinquencies, abandonments, or any other means, plus land that can be easily purchased, then subdivide it into truly small but developable parcels, and give it away to low- and moderate-income people – very much including new immigrants from Asia, Central America, and the Middle East – with the stipulation that they must build a home on the parcel within two years. Housing need not be the only use: small businesses and industries would be okay as well, as long as there is also a residence. One property per "customer" and no agglomeration of properties permitted. No public right-of-way could be wider than 50, maybe 40, feet. The maximum parcel size would be 2,000 square feet, which would yield 22 dwellings an acre, enough to support public transit. Resale would not be possible for a number of years. And if you don't develop your parcel within two years, you lose it. Once developed, there would be local tax revenues. Building and design advice would be available to those who wanted it. For many people, the prospect of owning property would be a dream come true, a fresh start. A one-storey, 1,000-square-foot house could be built on half of the lot, leaving the other 1,000 square feet for food gardening. Or one could make and sell things on one floor and live on the floor above. This is old-fashioned urban. There is nothing particularly new or drastic about the proposal. Such ideas were put in place long ago as active programs in so-called underdeveloped urban environments. Maybe that's what Cleveland is now. We need only admit it.

If Cleveland and other cities like it had taken their population losses and had not permitted an unsustainable sprawl over fine productive land, but had slowly and purposefully rebuilt truly urban environments on the once-developed land, then new, strong alternative ways of building might not be necessary. But as long as we're open to spreading and to an ever-expanding hole in the center of what was once a city, then some alternative ways of thinking and doing are in order. Civic pride alone would suggest the appropriateness and the potential richness of cleaning up the vacant land and the dereliction, and the planting of trees in a variety of old and new patterns. And what if, amid some of those new forests, people lived in small, tight, modest homes and set up businesses as well? The potential is wonderful.

Caprano

The Etcher of Caprano

Ettore was born in the small city of Caprano, not far from Naples, in the hills. Early he was drawn to etching. Caprano had a modest but long-standing reputation as a center of fine engraving and etching, the legacy of the artistic passions of an early duke who had brought to his employ and to his city the best engravers that he could afford. Families of engravers still lived there, although the duke was long gone; and while it would be too much to say that the craft flourished in Caprano (very little did), it can be said at least that it remained.

Not much else remained in Caprano. Like so many other small cities of the south – large hill towns, really – the Caprano community did not thrive. It was largely a farming community: olives, grapes, vegetables. And it was a minor administrative center. Starting with the end of the big war, the town council found it increasingly difficult to make ends meet, to keep things up. Young people left for Naples or Rome or the larger industrial or business centers of the north. Even then the townspeople would look to the possibility of outsiders, a great benefactor, or tourists to save them. Monies and projects from the central government were never enough or were ill placed. They knew it would always be so. The town leaders read about the tourists who flocked each summer to the northern cities, large and small, and dreamed of being discovered themselves.

But there wasn't much to discover. Caprano was like so many other hill cities. There were the old city gates and the remnants of medieval stone walls that crept intermittently along the hillside. There was no point in doing anything with them. Inside the main gate, outside of which was a small, long, and narrow park that looked over the valley, the main street rose steadily, though circuitously, to the top and then down again to a less used gateway, the "back" of the town. The width of the street was irregular, as were its directions, but mostly it was narrow, lined with three- and four-storey buildings, but even in the tightest places two cars could pass each other if their drivers were careful. There were no curbs; people and cars shared the street. The other streets were for the most part smaller versions of the main street: narrow and not-so-narrow streets lined with stone buildings of two or three floors with small, flat, open areas every now and then, off which might be a still smaller street or walk that gained access to more houses. The stone was a light, buff color with just the slightest touch of light red to it. Most of the buildings were of this stone, though some might be covered with stucco, a fashion that came some centuries ago. There were few stores on the smaller streets, though there were workshops. Most of the stores lined the main street and the main town square.

None of this was special. Nor were the convent, the market square, the main city piazza with the town hall where most people gathered, the churches, and the old castle, off to one side at the highest point in the city, which was in disrepair. None of the churches was by a renowned architect; the main one, Romanesque in origin, had been pretty well botched in an attempt to convert it to Baroque. There were no famous frescoes or statues. The first church of Caprano, San Ignazio, from the 11th century, remained at the edge of the city and the end of a street. It had a modest, paved, flat area in front and overlooked the fields beyond. Increasingly there were vacant buildings and, off the main street, some boarded-up stores.

Ettore grew up on the streets and in the spaces of Caprano, and in the countryside around it. He was a part of the city's rhythm, its daily and seasonal ritual dances – family times, public times, festival times, walking and talking times, times alone and times with others, posturing times, seasons, school times, eating times. In all of these he was much like everyone else, growing up and being a part of Caprano. His uniqueness was in his gift, his inherent understanding, his oneness with line and ink, and with the metals and stones and tools and acids of engraving, of etching. In this he was blessed. He was blessed, too, with a fine hand and with patience. Even as a young student he enjoyed working and reworking a plate, etching it, burnishing it, erasing it, changing the image from light to dark and back again, experimenting with the inks, repeating, repeating, until it was right – to his teachers and to Ettore himself. He could spend hours examining etching papers; feeling, looking, experimenting. And Ettore could paint. It came easily to him. At first, when he was young, his subjects were anything and everything: his home, his family, the countryside, his imagination. But most of all, he drew and painted and did etchings of Caprano. In time he would come to know every street, every piazza, every public and many not-so-public places. People watched him work. He talked with them and they came to know each other.

In a city known for the quality of its etchers and printing, young Ettore stood out. His gifts were apparent. Even then the firmness of his hand, his mastery of materials, his inventiveness with combinations of techniques announced the arrival of a very special talent. In everything else he was much like any other boy growing up in Caprano. Few were well off in Caprano, but they knew how to make do, to enjoy what there was to enjoy and to smile about the rest.

Ettore could learn only so much in Caprano. If he and his art were to progress, then he would need to study with master engravers. The place to do that was Rome. He was only 16 when he was admitted to the most prestigious *academie* of engraving in the capital, the one behind the Trevi Fountain. He would not have been able to go had it not been for the generosity of an uncle in whose house he was able to live across the river in Trastevere. Ettore – not immediately comfortable in Rome, where he knew almost no one, and a bit unsure of what he would find at the academy – threw himself into his work.

Whether Ettore found Lauro Bruno or Bruno discovered Ettore is unclear, and perhaps of no importance; but the fact that Ettore came under the influence of the older man was central to his development. Bruno was a senior professor at the academy and known to be among the two or three best etchers and printers in Italy. With the most complex, dark etchings, he was unsurpassed. He might work on a plate for days on end, changing it, knowing the print he had in mind, finally producing blacks that were impossibly deep, yet warm. The smallest highlights would shine, somehow showing just enough light, as if they were reflections, to capture surfaces and reveal form. And he lived to teach, to find someone to work with who understood and cared about this magical art and craft. So he and Ettore became close. In time he took Ettore to his studio in Testaccio, a small converted two-room, fourth-floor apartment on the Via Della Robia. He shared with Ettore all that he had done, including a series of maybe 400 etchings that had as their subject matter the smallest parts of the female form: a nostril, an ear, that mysterious, impossible-to-pinpoint spot where the breasts begin to rise, usually set off by a necklace or pendant or jewel with an inner life of its own. It was as if all the sensuality of all women was to be found in one small, focused area of the body. Ettore was stunned and was determined to know how to understand and do such work. Bruno was overjoyed at working with him. On days when Bruno was printing, for himself, and sometimes for fellow artists in order to make ends meet, Ettore would help him. And so he learned even more about printing and inks. In July, when Rome is so hot and humid, they might work for days on end, stripped save for their underwear and aprons.

Bruno knew Rome, almost every street in the historic center and a lot more as well. In his younger days he had walked it all, just as Ettore had walked Caprano. Once a week, they walked together and sometimes worked in the field. Though he missed his own city, Ettore came to know and to feel more than comfortable in Rome. Mostly he liked Rome in the fall and winter. There were fewer tourists then. He could walk the streets in greater comfort and be more leisurely in the museums and libraries. The daily life was more the life of Romans, doing whatever they did in their own city, especially in Trastevere, with its small shops, old buildings, local bars and cafés. When spring and summer came, it wasn't only the numbers of tourists that changed the city; the inhabitants seemed different, too, more with an eye to the strangers than to themselves. But Rome absorbed the tourists well enough, as it had been doing for centuries. It was a big city. Once, Ettore went to Florence, to study some etchings at the Uffizi, but he disliked it. Everything, it seemed, was for tourists. Where was Florence?

His work progressed. In time, just as he had been marked as special in Caprano, with special gifts, he became recognized in Rome. He had learned his lessons well. No one, it was said around the academy, except for Lauro Bruno years earlier, had achieved such results with the few Piranesi plates with which only the most senior and most gifted were permitted to work. Ettore was becoming more and more interested in color. Bruno knew that the best person in the world in multiple-color, large-size etching and printing was an old colleague now based in the United States. So, after four years in Rome, following a short visit back home, Ettore went to New York, to continue his education and development.

Except for the continued growth of his art and craft, it was not the best of times for him. Neither New York nor any other of the large cities that he visited in America was a comfortable place for Ettore to be. To be sure, there was vigor and excitement, and there were creative, talented people, but there was no time to think, to move with deliberation, to get to understand and be one with the surroundings, with place. And it was so hard to get to the country, which was not just a short walk or even a long walk from the city. And, it seemed to Ettore, it was such a terrible waste the way buildings and almost everything else were built for the moment, not for time, but for today's style and for show, to arrest the eye by shock. He preferred the small towns and came to know that he would return to Caprano.

He did indeed return to Caprano. In the world of etching and printing it was clear that a new master had arrived, someone so strong, so powerful, so creative as to change and redirect a whole art form, with new ways of seeing and expressing and doing, all grounded in the highest standards of craftsmanship. Ettore preferred to work alone, quietly. It was not difficult to find inexpensive, vacant space to rent and he took a large, ground-floor space on one of the small streets off the main piazza. Caprano remained a poor city. Not much had changed in the years since he had left, except perhaps that the finances and the upkeep of the town were a bit worse; things always seemed a bit worse.

Ettore was something of a hero to the city, someone to be proud of. He had traveled, had been to America, was a man of the world as well as a noted craftsman. As such a highly regarded person, though still young, the town sought his advice. Mostly, they wanted to find ways to help bring money and more life back to Caprano. They continued to look to the possibilities of tourism. What had Ettore found in his travels that could help them? He always counseled them to do only what they could do well: to farm; to do fine printing and engraving;

perhaps to develop a small, high-quality paper industry because there would always be a demand for good paper, but be careful about the use of water and pollution. And he suggested the making of new types of presses: there would be a need for large, precision presses that made use of new technologies, and for parts. He cautioned against tourism. Catering to tourists, he said, would change their city, change the people. Had they seen what had happened to Sorrento? It was no longer possible to have a good meal there. The restaurants catered to German and English tourists, with German and English menus, perhaps the two worst cuisines in the world.

He recalled a visit to Santa Fe, in New Mexico, an historic small city now known for its art, galleries, and the preservation of its physical history. He had gone there to talk with engravers meeting at a well-known art institute. Tourism might have been good for the city finances, but it had left Santa Fe more a place for visitors than for local residents. No one, it seemed, lived in the center. New buildings, in old adobe styles, seemed made of plastic. Seeing Native Americans lined up and selling jewelry along an old, historic building was, for Ettore, depressing. In Caprano, he advised, they should do for themselves. If visitors wanted to come, that would be all right; but don't change the city for them. The townspeople listened.

Although he worked in all the usual formats of etching, Ettore also worked large, as large and then larger than people had worked before in quality printing. This required new papers and new presses. He made them himself or adapted what he could find to meet his needs. The influence of Lauro Bruno on his early work was sometimes clear, but now it was at a grand new scale, and in color. He won awards at the most prestigious annual competitions, and with the awards came more commissions. Over the years his work became sought after, both his etchings and his paintings. No one had captured light as he had, especially the light in shadows. He brought fame to himself and to his community. Young and then older artists wanted to see his work and see how he worked. He remembered what Bruno had done for him, so he permitted them to come and talked with them as they watched him work. But he nearly always worked alone. Only Bruno worked with him – on the rare occasions, perhaps once every two or three years, when he visited.

Nothing much changed in Caprano. It was a little poorer, or at least the townspeople said it was. Ettore lived a quiet life. To be sure, two or three times a day he would go to the central piazza for a drink and a pastry, and he would talk with his friends. He was always at the festivals. He took his walk, with the others, on Sunday afternoons. He was friendly, though shy, with women. He painted more, and demand for his paintings increased. As the years passed, two things happened: Caprano became poorer and Ettore became more renowned. The city still thought of tourists. Ettore still counseled them not to. Then, although no one could pinpoint exactly when, Caprano began to change, to prosper. At the heart of it, Ettore caused it to happen. The quality of his work and the way he worked put Caprano on the map.

It helped that Caprano had a long-standing tradition as a center of etching. Its craftsmen and artists began to do well; they came, after all, from what had now become known as the Caprano "school." So their work, too, was sought after, and they were indeed artists of quality. Soon, others came, to learn from Ettore and from the other Caprano craftsmen. The new printing methods brought people to see and study them, slowly, over time. At first, vacant buildings were rented at reasonable prices. Some work rooms found new tenants. Later, the artists and craftsmen were followed by people who wanted to live near them, to be associated with them somehow, to gain stature merely by being in the same place.

An international paper company, from France, seeing the value of challenging the famous northern Italian Fabriano firm in its own country, sponsored a major week-long festival in Caprano, to show its newest products, especially the largest fine-quality etching papers to be found, and to have exhibits of work in any number of print-making categories. Another year they brought world-famous artists to Caprano for a month to experiment with and show the possibilities of paper, culminating in the festival. The artists came, and with them visitors.

There was an intense creative period, lasting perhaps five years, of great experimentation and creativity in Caprano. And though the high quality of the work continued, changes came with the visitors and tourists. The two or three small, modest hotels were joined by two or three others, in converted old houses. Then two new ones: the first on the edge of the city, cleverly integrating remnants of the old city walls into its design; and the second a resort with a pool and tennis courts. Restaurants changed, were open longer, became more expensive. In time, postcards and souvenirs appeared. Buildings were reconditioned, modernized. Some rents increased. Caprano became cleaner than it had been. Ettore saw new people at the bar. Those his age, now not so young, came less often or went to places down the hill, near that gate at the back of the town.

For the visitors, the biggest attraction was Ettore. They wanted to see him, see this famous man at work, perhaps catch his eye. Ettore's studio, his workplace, like so many others, was open to the street. He worked inside and was visible. People would line up on the street to watch him at work. He disliked it, but Caprano was his home. There were times when his doors remained closed, but still the people came. He painted more, not in his workplace but in the countryside, in remote parts of the city, and in the neighboring town. His hours changed. All of this did not happen at once, but over time.

Caprano was thriving. There was talk of restoring the church, back to its original design, but doing it right this time. In a year or so there would be enough money. The old castle on the hill became an expensive inn, and its courtyards proved to be a better setting for small stores than anything to be found in America, or so some of the tourists said. It did very well. Masons and plasterers and building craftsmen also did well. More and more people discovered the simplicity and beauty of Caprano.

When he had been in America, Ettore had visited the little city of Carmel, in California. He had not felt comfortable there. It was possible for a city to be too clean, too right, too precious. Self-awareness was everywhere. When he went to see the Giottos in Assisi, to the north, he found many of the same qualities. Now he was less and less comfortable in his own community; and it was he, through the quality of his own work, who had been responsible for it becoming all that he did not want it to be. He was no longer young. None of his options, it seemed to Ettore, were good: he could stay in Caprano, which was really no longer his Caprano; or he could leave, with the remote possibility that some balance would return, but with the sadness of being cut off from his roots.

Ettore remembered Lauro Bruno, who by now had passed away, in Rome and his Testaccio studio. In the most simple, crowded quarters, Bruno's creativity was able to find outlet. Similar places to work could be found there. Maybe Ettore should leave his home again, not this time to learn his craft and hopefully not for ever, but for a period. What had been found could be unfound. Maybe, before his time would come, Caprano would be unfound, the wave would pass, and Ettore would return.

Liberty Bakery

At 12.45, on a gray, rainy Friday afternoon in early August, there are six people in line waiting to be served in the Liberty Bakery, Vancouver. The entry door is on East 21st Avenue, not on Main Street, the more trafficked business street where it might be expected. Upon entering, there are three steps down to the counter where customers' orders are taken. The space is small, with baked goods, cookies, and sandwiches displayed behind a glass counter to the left and shelves with various breads behind that. Behind the counter where the orders are taken are shelves with plates, cups, a coffee maker, and a large soup pot. To the left, beyond an open doorway, is the bakery and space to wash dishes. At a small table to the right of the three steps, a middle-aged to elderly lady is sitting. Further to the right, through a short passage, is the main room, for dining. On this day there are 23 chairs loosely located at six or seven tables and all but one or two are occupied.

Liberty Bakery is first about making and selling fine baked goods at reasonable prices, but it is also about being part of and making community, and doing so consciously. The prices and the community-making are related. "Liberty" is the name of the lady seen sitting at the table aside the entrance. She is the owner, along with her baker husband, and perhaps other family members. She was born of an Italian mother and a father from Central America. The husband is from Sweden. Earlier, he or they had a bakery in the Kitsilano neighborhood, to the west, where, on some afternoons, they still walk along the shoreline. The walls of the front, dining room display 35 pictures of Rome, taken by a daughter on a recent trip. The exhibit is a sharing of this momentous visit with the community. In another month or so these pictures will be replaced by other art, locally produced.

The front room is informally arranged with simple, wood-topped tables on metal bases. Designs have been cut into the wooden tops and they are painted with a mix of colors. The chairs, too, are informal and easily moved. Patrons carry their food into this room from the counter, where they order and pay for it. What stands out is that there is no door to Main Street. There are, though, glass windows, so people can look out to the street. Almost certainly there was once a door. Aside the entry on East 21st Avenue, on the sidewalk, there are normally five tables, but not today because of the rain.

On this Friday the front room is crowded, mostly women of many ages, some kids, and a few men. People move the chairs around, as needed, and as they become available. Waiting to give my order, I wonder where I might sit. At the front window there is a table with a single empty chair; a possibility. But a young lady, part of a group of four, takes it, stands at it, surveys possibilities, and, when two more chairs become available, lightly peruses and moves them to the table. Other people move to allow her to make the shift. One more chair to go. Her friends arrive with their food. Back in front of the cookie case, two kids survey the possibilities, back and forth. One asks the price of some cookies. She has enough money to buy two.

The red-haired lady behind the counter asks if I want my order – black bean soup with lime chilies (terrific, with a bite), a ham and cheese focaccia, and tea – to go or to eat there. She asks if I have a place to sit. She offers me the one where Liberty was sitting, which has a small "reserved" sign on it. Sitting at this privileged location, it is possible to see the comings and goings of customers, the various people at work, and the prices, to compare them with those of other bakeries. The baker, Liberty's husband, brings out a pumpkin pie that sells for $5.50. A slice costs a dollar and they will add whipped cream for free. Whole apple and cherry pies can be ordered for $5.50, too. Two women take orders, one young and another, black, who seems to be in her forties. They also wash dishes and clear tables. An older, Asian man, perhaps in his late sixties, is in and out of the kitchen–bakery and has been cleaning some pots. He brings out a pot of soup to replace an empty one. Liberty is now behind the counter. More baked goods appear, including a lemon swirl cake that sells for $7.70, and a Swedish cake for $6.00, or $1.50 a slice. All of these prices are much cheaper than those at other fine bakeries, of which there are many in Vancouver. A banana bread or carrot cake is $5.50. I decide to try a piece of the newly arrived pumpkin pie; a very good decision.

At 1.15 there are six people in line, waiting to order. At the counter there is a bowl for tips, with a note that says the money will go to a heart–stroke foundation, for charity. This suggests that the employees are adequately paid, without the need for tips to make ends meet, and that there is compassion for people who need help. Behind the counter is a poster-sized letter on the wall from grade five at David Livingston School, thanking the Liberty Bakery for its contribution toward the school trip to Barberville.

Low prices here are at least in part a matter of policy. They know their prices are low. I am reminded of a bar in Rome, the Calisto, immediately around a corner from Piazza Santallaria in Trastavere, at the start of the Via San

Francesco a Ripa, on its way to Piazza San Francesco d'Assisi. The restaurants and bars that line the piazza and beyond are not cheap, catering as they do to tourists and the generally well-to-do. The ice cream, coffee, and brioche at Bar Calisto are, by comparison, inexpensive. It is more than the turning of the corner that accounts for the price differential and more than the less fashionable and less well-maintained physical surroundings. It has been and is a matter of ideology, of remaining local, of being part of a local community and encouraging its continuance. A losing battle? Perhaps, but why would a local person go elsewhere? At Liberty Bakery, the prices, the simple décor, the employees, the general low-key civility, and the participation in the community all suggest that this is much more than a place of business. Liberty's daughter, the clerk–waitress with the red hair, confirms the messages given off by the place. The store hours, as well, are instructive: Mondays to Fridays from 8.00 to 6.00; Saturdays and Sundays from 8.00 to 5.00; and all holidays from 8.00 to 4.00. A living part of the community, all the time.

On a better day, a warm, sunny Saturday morning in summer, the kind that makes one forget that it rains a lot in Vancouver, we sit outside, at one of the five tables along the sidewalk. With others, we drink our coffee or tea and eat a goodie or two. The other tables are taken but when we arrive there always seems to be a space, for others as well. People may read the paper. Across the street there is a wall mural of a one-storey house of the type that one might see in Italy. There are three parking spaces along the curb, but most people arrive on foot. People pass by or enter the bakery. Inside, there are seven people waiting at the counter. Most will come outside; a delightful place to be.

Stopping By

Dan stopped by the other afternoon; Dan Richman. Dan's a friend. We met a couple of years ago when Elizabeth and I were looking for a contractor to remake the deck that hangs high above the ground outside our living room. I had stopped in at the hardware store on 24th Street, Tuggey's, told them what I was after, and they gave me his name and phone number, adding that he was a good guy, did fine work, and that his charges were reasonable. All of that proved true, and led to other jobs, as well as friendship.

On the afternoon that he stopped by, we spent a couple of hours shooting the breeze while I prepared food for a group of students who would be coming for dinner. We talked about his daughter, in India as part of a semester abroad program, about why I was talking to realtors to get a sense of what the house was worth in case we wanted to move, about our lady loves, about his plans not to do more building work himself but to be a "real" contractor, directing the work of others, and about what should be done on our house. Dan's a writer, a poet, and once taught at Chabot College and San Francisco City College. We've done two readings together at the local Glen Park bookstore, Bird and Beckett. Dan's latest is a prose memoir about his grandmother, his mom and dad, and other family members while growing up in the Bronx. His writing is very good, especially when he reads it aloud; a listener can feel the people and visualize the streets. We tasted some liquors, to see what might go best on a fruit salad I was preparing. Some students arrived, and soon after I went to pick up Elizabeth at the BART station. Dan stayed until we returned and then he left.

People, friends, don't just stop by unannounced any more. Dan's visit, it occurs to me, may be the first time in 40 years, since moving to San Francisco from the East, that a friend has just stopped by, not for any particular reason, but to see a liked person and shoot the breeze. Out of the blue! "I was in the neighborhood and thought I'd stop by." Does anyone else do that any more? Sure, Matthew, in high school and junior high, used to stop by at the Mazzolas', across the street. Maybe to see Anthony; more likely to get a free bowl of pasta from Tony and Stella before our own dinner. (The Mazzolas ate early.) And there were times when Tony crossed the street to our house, but usually there was some purpose for his visits: like he had seen a stranger at our door the other day. Our impromptu socializing was done on the street. When Glen Gobar knocks on the door, it's for a reason: to tell us he wants to have some trees trimmed and to ask if we mind; or to let us know that he and Ann will be away for a week, and to ask if we would look in on his house every now and then. Niko tells me that he stops by one or two of his neighbors with some frequency; but that sometimes he gets a sense that one friend's wife might not be too happy when he does so because she'll go somewhere else in the house soon after his arrival. He says that Janet does the same thing when his neighbor stops by unannounced. These are social encounters among neighbors who live very close to one another.

In Pittsburgh, many years ago, Ed Tucker might stop by unannounced. He'd come by car or on foot. I remember a particular Saturday morning when he showed up with Jerry Stern and we took a drive and walk upriver from the old Pennsylvania Railroad Station. I think we were looking for wall paneling. Dave Amstey might ring the doorbell on a weekend day; and, at night, Dick Hazley might show up after one of his hypnotism performances at an Elks Club or a Veteran of Foreign Wars social. In turn, we might drop by the Tuckers' house on a Sunday afternoon, just to talk with Ed and Rita, maybe have a few words with Uncle Hen and inspect the refrigerator in his bedroom, where he kept his supply of beer and other spirits. They'd either be home or not and if they were home we'd quickly know if it was convenient to come in. If it wasn't, no problem. It wouldn't stop us calling another time. Stopping by was usually a spur-of-the-moment decision. We'd find ourselves in a friend's neighborhood, not too far from where he or she lived, and say, "Hmm, maybe it would be nice to see Ed," or Tom and Barnaby Davidson, or Jerry, and we'd stop by. I often walked over to Izzy and Charlotte Cohen's house and Izzy came over to ours on the spur of the moment, often in the summer, to our small back yard. There is no recollection of what we talked about. True, in Pittsburgh, Bernie Chodin would often stop by, unannounced, usually on a weekday evening. He was something of a pain in the ass and it was hard to get him to leave without being insulting. So I'd be insulting. But it never stopped him coming back.

Earlier still, before Pittsburgh days, people, mostly cousins, would stop by at my grandparents' apartments in the Bronx, almost always on Saturday afternoons. I don't think prearrangements were made for these visits; at least I never heard of any. Refreshments were always served. Maybe everyone just knew that Grandma made rugalah and other pastries for weekends and they were very good, especially with tea. On a particular spring Saturday, Jimmy Sanders stopped by and before long he was showing us the diamonds he carried with him. He wasn't working, wouldn't think of it on the Sabbath, but had all these diamonds wrapped in small, black velvet packages inside of brown wrapping paper that could fit into the inside breast pocket of his long black coat. He worked in the diamond industry, perhaps as a courier, and carried diamonds around with him. During World War II, Jimmy had been drafted into the army, which was okay by him as long as he could remain strictly kosher in his eating. He was sent for training to Kentucky, where his mom and others sent him food packages with great regularity to keep him going. Jimmy said prayers every morning, complete with phylacteries; his mostly Kentucky and other southern comrades in arms thought he was nuts. Ultimately, the army decided he was more trouble than he was worth and discharged him. So we spent an hour or so looking at diamonds, discussing his army days, and gaining news about his brother, Saul, who had given up trying to make it as an opera singer, had become a cantor, and was now somewhere in Texas where a congregation had hired him. Saul married a non-Jewish woman, perhaps the daughter of a Methodist minister, musically inclined, and the Sanders family sat Shiva for him; for them he had died. That was the sort of thing that you talked about when someone stopped by.

Uncle Morris had a friend, Eli, a so-called art dealer who might stop by on a Saturday or Sunday afternoon. He'd spent his childhood in a concentration camp in Europe, was smart as hell, knew how to get by, bought and sold paintings at auctions downtown, had a string of artists who produced "fine old paintings" that he sold, and was scared of no one. We'd walk up the Grand Concourse to a side-street coffee house that sold very thick Turkish coffee and very sweet pastry that he liked, talk about his art dealings, troubles with a judge who wanted him to pay alimony to an estranged wife, and then go our separate ways.

Do most people even think about stopping by these days? I suspect that it doesn't enter the realm of possibility for most people. Or maybe it's just the people I know, in the circles I travel, who don't stop by: it would be bad manners, intrusive, awkward for the persons being called upon. What if they were busy, or had other guests? They could always say they were busy, or had guests. Why would it matter if they were friends? Now people call before they contemplate coming by, usually days in advance. Or do they even do that very much – that is, invite themselves over, say tomorrow or next Saturday? With cell phones, stopping by could be instantaneous, or almost so. But no one has ever done that with us: "Hey, Jake, I'm in the neighborhood. Okay if I stop by?" Why not?

For Elizabeth and me there are special activities that are a bit like stopping by. There are particular farmers at the Alemany Market who we always buy from and talk to, Saturday morning: Victor, who sells fresh and dried fruit; Andrea, who comes all the way from Ojai with avocados, lemons, and mangos; the fingerling-potato farmer who reminds us that his cherries will be coming soon and that he will put some aside for us; Al, the huge Samoan with the great melons, tomatoes, and peppers; and, more recently, Fumi, whose flowers last two to three weeks, who inherited her farm from her parents, both of whom died of cancer. We regularly overbuy from these people and others, but it's about more than buying: we talk about cooking and weather and rents, too. It's important not to buy everything we need at the farmers' market so that we can stop once or twice each week at the Church and 30th Street greengrocer to talk with the Greek lady cashier, now that she's back after a long stay with her dying mother. Knowing and talking with the guys at Tuggey's hardware store is, after all, how we met Dan. Stopping by to see Augustino and Carmen at Tomasso's is much more than a matter of eating. It's a chance to catch up with friends. This, I think, is what community is all about.

We must stop weekly at Lucca's on Valencia Street. Second only in importance to the pastas, sauces, oils, cheeses, wines, frittatas, olives, mortadella, focaccia, calamari salad, and other goodies were the discussions with Alfio about recipes, where he would eat that night, his last vacation trip or the next one, and talks with Michael about wine, or with Martin. Alfio always sent his regards to Elizabeth. I say "sent" because one day Alfio wasn't there and there was a picture of him in the window and another next to the counter. He had had a heart attack and died over the weekend. Big sadness. Big talking about Alfio for many weeks with the guys.

I love to walk up Kearney Street with Elizabeth, to stop across from the Coppola Building, look up to a bay window on the third floor and shout, at the top of my voice, "Cheryl. It's me, Jake, come on down!" She opens the window, laughing, feigning embarrassment, and waves.

All those people at the market and in the stores, and stops at Cheryl's, are truly important stopping bys, but they are different from Dan's visit.

Perhaps people in small communities, especially in the continental heartland and in the South, still stop by, even today. Neighborhoods where people walk a lot, as a normal way of getting around, might engender more spontaneous visits than those where people do almost all of their travel by car. But Dan's stopping by was by car and strikes me as being memorable. He doesn't live too far away, but I've never been to his house. I don't even know for sure where it is. Now, though, I'll have to find the exact address so that some day, if the mood strikes, I might stop by.

Curitiba and the Making of Community

In late 1974, after but a one-day visit to Curitiba, Brazil, it was possible to think that this might be a city with a very different trajectory than other major and more known cities in the country: Rio de Janeiro, São Paolo, Belo Horizonte, and, of course, Brasilia. There are few cities with the setting, physical charm, spectacular beaches, and fine old downtown of Rio de Janeiro. And there were then, now too, few as intense and bustling, and bursting out and up, as São Paolo. Belo Horizonte seemed a large, mineral-based industrial city trying to grapple with growth and congestion issues. Brasilia, new then and not so old now, was more a lonely diagram than a city. Curitiba, much smaller than the others, with about 650,000 people at the time, capital of the agriculturally based state of Parana, was significantly different than the others, even at a glance, not so much in its smaller size, but in the newness of some improvements and those, one would soon find, planned for the future. There was an auto-free downtown crowded with people, some fine and well-maintained old parks and squares, and major visible efforts at new citywide parks, some near the periphery. This was a stark contrast to roadways being built in at least one park in São Paolo at the time. There were details such as an old glue factory that had been turned into a creativity center for all the arts, and one heard about a new industrial estate to attract economic investment. There was a strong concept plan for future growth and development of the city, basically in the form of a diagram. The plan demanded five major transportation corridors, called structurals, radiating out from a strong central downtown, along which high-density, high-rise development was encouraged. The central road of each corridor, built almost entirely using existing streets, was focused on a transit-only busway, to encourage public transit use and discourage autos. Land between the structurals was to be low-density development, large parks, and other public uses. It was a very simple

Flower Street

plan and one that was immediately visible. This was very different than what could be seen not only in other Brazilian cities, but in most cities of the world. This was taking a well-established city and seriously planning a new and different future; and, as a visitor might later find out, consciously making community.

Making community, not from scratch, but in long-established urban areas, especially in the 20th and 21st centuries, doesn't just happen. It takes people and their individual and collective decisions and efforts. In the case of Curitiba, the work was clearly directed by the Mayor, Jaime Lerner, and a group of close colleagues, very much including Fani Lerner, Jaime's wife. Having had the plan ideas explained and some of the early realities shown to me during a Saturday morning, by Lerner and a few staff, I was at the performance of a wonderful young folk singer that evening in an intimate public venue, a hall recently transformed from a military powder magazine. And there was Lerner with his wife, talking, talking, talking with lots of people, laughing, enjoying. We nodded to each other from a distance. I had been a bit skeptical about who he might be and what he represented. Mayors of capital cities in Brazil at that time were appointed by a military government. But his informality and ease that evening, just as it had been with many eager and known greeters at the Paseo Publico park that noon, for snacks, seemed without pretension. He and his colleagues seemed "real." His four-year term as Mayor would soon expire and, though much had already been done, I wondered what the future would bring.

Back in Berkeley, Curitiba, its positivism and its differences from other cities with which I was familiar, stayed in my mind. Two years later, Lerner was invited to Berkeley as a visiting instructor. Toward the end of his stay he was invited to serve a second term as Mayor, but he fulfilled his commitment to the university which gave him a chance, unpressured, to think of what new things might be appropriate the second time around. In turn, I was invited back to Curitiba many times, to act as part consultant/part informal go-between to Lerner and the staff of the more official planning body of the city.

It was of more than passing interest to watch Lerner and his group at work, developing programs and projects. Quite often the work day would start not at city hall but at the headquarters building of the park department, a new building in a new park. There seemed to be a constant review, all morning, of new and developing ideas, some by young designers, others by more established colleagues. An idea, say, for a new small-scale commercial area along a street, or the conversion of an old lumber yard into a market that would sell only cheap "seconds" (clothes by the kilo), for low- and moderate-income people, or evening food markets on the streets, or a small park or housing scheme, or something much more grand. All these and more would be briefly presented, reviewed, dropped or taken further. It was a creative way to spend a morning, to be followed by a family lunch at home, and then on to city hall and all the other requirements of being Mayor.

The future, at least the next 25 years, would see truly impressive changes to Curitiba: physical changes, social changes, economic changes, environmental changes. During that period, Curitiba can be likened to an ideas factory – ideas to be emulated and expanded. And many of those ideas started, as well they should, with a plan.

Lerner and his team had come to office as a group of architects and designers, albeit with social do-good intentions. The team had already spent time on their own drafting what could be called a structural plan for the city. So he and they came into office with strong ideas of what they wanted to do: the linear transportation plan, the strong center tied to high-density development, the open-space system. They would build from and upon those ideas.

Curitiba was about 150 years old in the 1970s. It is about 45 minutes southwest of Rio and São Paolo by air. The population, which would grow to over 1.5 million people by 1990, was diverse, with many people who had roots in Poland, Italy, Germany, other Eastern European countries, and Japan, as well as native Brazilians. Lerner had a strong sense of social responsibility, aided and abetted by his wife. Early on, one heard such phrases as: "The city is a place for encounter"; "People have to feel there is potential, poor and well-to-do alike"; and "People have to feel that basic needs are being addressed."

On that first trip to Curitiba we stopped on Flower Street, the main downtown street, which had been pedestrianized. There was a long piece of paper running along the center of the street, with pieces of wood every half meter, holding it down. And there were lots of kids painting whatever they wished on the sections. Earlier, the transition to a pedestrian street had taken place over a 72-hour period. Some merchants were opposed to the change and threatened to drive there over the busy weekend. That was why the children's painting strip had been initiated. Who would dare to drive where kids, watched by their parents, were painting? In short order, the merchants were calling for the pedestrian area to be expanded. More importantly, the Saturday morning painting strip was still happening in the 1990s, and may still be happening now. Kids of all economic backgrounds painted together; the making of community.

In all, Lerner served three four-year terms as Mayor, non-consecutively. In 1989, after the national government had changed, he was elected, rather than appointed. Saul Raiz, a friend, was Mayor between his first and second terms. Raphael Greca and Cassio Tanaguchi, two close colleagues, followed Lerner after his final term. Lerner himself went on to be elected twice to the governorship of the state.

The list of programs and projects initiated and carried out by Lerner and his colleagues over the 25-plus years that they held office in Curitiba is as diverse as it is long. Those already noted are impressive enough, but in addition there was the "House of Memories," an effort run mostly by young people which aimed to solicit from citizens old photos of families and buildings, essays, articles, family histories, anything of the past that related to the city and its people. The gathered material was filed, ingeniously, in filing cabinets above an old hardware store in the historic city center to provide an accessible archive.

From this archive it became possible to produce, at very short notice, small publications to highlight neighborhood festivals, family celebrations, building histories, physical as well as social histories. In short, it provided a means to inform residents about their city and its people; to make community. Perhaps that project is less remembered now. It was important then.

Curitiba was best known for its public transportation system. It evolved mightily over the period in question. Though dependent on public transportation, the plan was integrated with the auto, but not with freeways. It is basically a lineal city concept but with a strong city center. Each of the "structurals" has a central roadway for express buses along with side access lanes for local traffic and parking. One-way streets, one block away from and generally parallel to the central route, are for autos but also for non-local buses. The land between the one-way streets is for very high-density development, to encourage transit accessibility and use, while land outside the "structurals" is for low-density uses, mostly housing. The system is not publicly owned. Rather, a conglomerate of private companies operates as would a public system via city controls of the routes, stops, fares, transfer locations, colors of the buses, and lettering. Over time, development has indeed followed the "structurals," with usage of approximately 25,000 people per day in 1974 growing to almost a million per day in 1993. In time, commercial facilities were integrated with major outlying terminals, as were community centers. At one point in the 1990s there was a 28 percent increase in transit users who had previously used autos (although in later years, after 2000, it seems that some of this usage has not held up).

Perhaps the most significant positive changes to the system were the long, double-articulated buses and the locally invented boarding tubes, for rapid entry and exit. Volvo, with a local presence, was persuaded to build these buses, capable of handling 300 passengers. The attractive, transparent boarding tubes, whose sliding doors could be coordinated with sliding bus doors, are raised to the level of the bus's floor. A patron pays the fare to enter the tube, which is on the sidewalk, facilitating rapid entry and exit from the bus. The result is an ability to run a bus every minute on a "structural," equating to transporting 18,000 people per hour – rapid transit volumes at a fraction of the cost of a subway, which the city could not afford.

Lerner and his colleagues knew that it was important to expand the city's economic base, too. They soon established an industrial park (albeit in too large an area) that attracted companies not through tax breaks but via efficient, one-stop permitting, a skilled workforce, and an international school for the children of foreign executives. At a far different scale, I remember visiting a downtown showroom that put merchants in direct contact with low-income craftspeople and their attractively displayed products. They also converted no longer usable buses into colorful traveling classrooms that taught stenography, electrical skills, computer skills, and so on to low-income people near where they lived. I still own some embroidered dish towels made from old coffee sacks, which Fani Lerner taught low-income women to make and market.

In the city center – behind building façades that had been "improved" with every kind of plastic and pressed-metal skins – were some fine, old, crafted and articulated structures. With the owners' permission, young staff showed how these buildings could be restored to their historic greatness. Far from all of them were subsequently restored, but enough were to make a difference. At the same time, the staff designed a simple, contiguous, glass-and-metal canopy that could be attached to buildings above doors and windows to gain some continuity and provide shelter from the rain. Blank building walls were painted with murals that showed what old buildings might once have looked like. Some of these still exist. Very inexpensive bus shelters were designed and built, as were extremely inexpensive new streetlights, little more than four globes attached to four thin and shaped aluminum pipes held together with metal straps. Essentially, from the start, the team worked within their means, on the cheap. If their means increased over time, and if the ideas and programs proved worthy and valuable, then the projects could be replaced, as needed, with more refined, longer-lasting ones. If what had been done proved to be of little value, then little would have been lost.

In the arena of social (and physical) infrastructure, Lerner's team started early on with a school-building program. From a simple, one-size-fits-all, utilitarian design, they built one-, two-, and three-storey schools, with the only apparent differences being the number of floors and the corner placement of staircases. Later, there were small libraries, called "lighthouses of learning," each of a similar design – recall the U.S. Carnegie libraries – and each with a lighthouse-like small tower to give it focus. Electronic connections to the world may be more important than book collections, but they are not more important to the buildings and to the making of community.

The city built childcare centers for the small kids of low-income working mothers in simple, undistinguished buildings. Visiting them, unannounced, I had never seen such attentive care of so many little ones (some as young as six months). Older kids, too, knew that they could come to these places after school, before their parents came home. Later, the city started a program to house abandoned children, mostly boys. Lerner and his wife had been robbed, at gunpoint, by some young kids in Rio. With the question of social responsibility ever before them, and with this Rio phenomenon arising in Curitiba too, they tried to do something about it. Bringing the kids to a clean-living situation, clothing and feeding them, was the Lerners' response. But, by law, the youths could not be kept in such places for more than a few days without their consent. So the idea was to make their stay one that would discourage a return to street life. I do not know how well the program worked in the long run. But the idea and its implementation speak of a social justice frame of mind.

With some notable exceptions, the housing programs were not as successful as other projects in the city. The low- and moderate-income housing schemes launched in the early 1980s were somewhat dismal: rows of non-descript, often gray, two- and three-storey blocks of flats, generally devoid of any landscape relief; overall, not too different from constructions one might see in São Paulo at the time.

However, new ideas and better designed housing would begin to appear in the mid-1980s, particularly through the city's housing agency, COHAB, headed by Raphael Dely. Young designers working for COHAB produced some fine moderate- and higher-density housing geared to creating real neighborhoods, including physical arrangements that encouraged people to meet each other and common gathering and play spaces. A self-help housing program was also developed, in which small plots were provided with basic utility connections where people could, by and large, build whatever they wished, with advice about design and materials provided by city staff. By the early 1990s it was also possible to see, not far from the central area of the city, handsome, small, two-storey structures, the ground floors of which were used for business – maybe craft-making, maybe by people who collected rags and other recyclables for disposal – with the top floors providing modest living units.

At one point they even experimented with the idea of "rurban villages," somewhat reminiscent in form of old New England villages. These comprised small, simple houses, close together, on very narrow but long parcels, facing a street or small green space near public transit. The intention was that people could farm those long parcels and produce at least enough food for themselves and hopefully some surplus for sale, while also having access to city job opportunities. They even experimented with trying to generate electricity from organic waste. This experiment cannot be called a success, but at least it was tried.

Between Lerner's second and third terms as Mayor, there was a growth of favelas, largely self-built squatters' settlements, for which Rio's hills are famous. They had not previously been common in Curitiba. At least one of them was on the large land area set aside for industrial development. They had been encouraged for political reasons by Lerner's predecessor, and represented both social and public health problems. These were messy places: poor, if any, utility infrastructure; drainage problems; uneven and unpaved pathways; catch-as-catch-can building materials. The city's public maintenance crews could not even get their equipment into them to perform basic services. What to do? The city wanted the areas cleaned, at least, and concluded that the best way to achieve this was through an exchange program. Any resident who managed to fill a large plastic bag (provided by the city) with refuse and brought it to a drop-off location at their nearest bus stop would be issued with a free bus ticket – something that poor people living far from the center both wanted and needed. The plan worked. The favelas became cleaner, if not middle-class clean, and less of a public health problem.

Meanwhile, the city seems to have taken advantage of every opportunity that presented itself to build a park. Park Iguacu exploited a flood-control project that involved construction of a new canal parallel to the River Iguacu. The canal–river park includes a public fish farm, free fishing opportunities, water trips on a small boat, a zoo, and even community orchards. Passauna Park is a regional facility at the city's edge that took advantage of a new reservoir. The city assumed control of the lake front and built a continuous path around it for hiking, with bridges, shelters, picnic spots, and a viewing tower. The initial stage of the transformation was completed in just 28 days.

Other parks, large and small, form a series of cultural gestures that celebrate community diversity. There are German and Italian entryways along roads, a Ukrainian park, and a Polish park, complete with replicas of old Polish village buildings, built to celebrate a visit by the Pope; lineal parks and bikeways along drainage canals and abandoned railroad lines; and neighborhood improvements including sidewalk widenings that have provided places for people to sit, play areas in the centers of wide streets, and skateboard parks at street intersections. All of these smallish projects were completed before similar projects became common in U.S. cities. Over a 20-year period, public open space in Curitiba increased from 0.5 square meters per person to 50 square meters per person, despite the rapid population growth.

The favela-improvement, parks, and open-space projects were all elements in a much larger undertaking directed toward environmental responsibility. To be sure, the emphasis on public transportation to reduce auto travel is a very significant part of that endeavor. The same is true of programs launched in the early 1980s to recycle and reuse waste. Kids at school were taught to put different types of waste in different containers and to urge their parents to do likewise. One could attend, on a Saturday morning – neighborhood festive gatherings that emphasized recycling, demonstrating the three types of container for waste that are now so common all over the world – and also see and buy products made from recycled waste that were beginning to appear. All of this was well before such programs became common in North America. It wasn't long before they were selling recyclable refuse to help defray costs, as well as promoting products that could be made from the materials collected. In the 1990s approximately 70 percent of households participated in the recycling of municipal solid waste through a number of novel programs, aided by public information and public advocacy.

What better way to advance understanding of the importance of the natural environment, and to encourage the fight against those forces that despoil land and water, than to build a small memorial to the memory of Chico Mendez, killed in the Amazon because of his environmental advocacy? The memorial was in the form of two or three Amazonian hut structures in a wooded, undeveloped area where weekend programs were held primarily for kids to learn how to sustain themselves for a few days. The participants become cognizant of the natural environment and learned to respect it. More simply, and earlier, the city improved access to the water from a natural spring by piping it to a more convenient, easily reached location. (Although, in a modest backfire, some locals still preferred to fill their containers directly from the original earth source. Who knew what devilish things might be done along that short length of pipe?)

In a much larger project, by the mid-1990s some 200,000 trees had been planted along public streets. Would that more had been planted along the "structurals," along the sidewalks, and even along the narrow lineal islands between the busways and access roads.

The so-called Free University of the Environment stands out as perhaps the most dramatic of the projects, even more so than the environmentally directed and large arboretum, which was also built as part of a park. With a basic structure made of old wooden telephone poles, a ramp winds upward, perhaps the equivalent of three or four floors, to a viewing platform from which much of the city can be seen. Along the ramp is a series of small classrooms within which courses on the environment are taught. They hang on the basic structure. On the ground, next to a pond, is a small amphitheater for outside events. All this is reached by a winding wooden pathway. The whole project was completed in two months, and has deservedly become a tourist stop.

Finally, mention should be made of the Arama Opera House, once known as the Wire Opera House. In need of a venue for a fast-approaching major theater festival, a glass-domed and glass-enclosed hall, made of long, bent metal tubes in the form of arches, was constructed in just 69 days. The location is an abandoned quarry, with the opera house reached by a simple bridge. The seats were indeed made of wire, with the floor consisting of rubber pads of the sort one sees in children's playgrounds. The tourist buses stop here, too. From that short entry bridge, looking down to the water below, a sharp-eyed visitor might just see a turtle.

For sure, not all of the projects worked or worked well. Basic street maintenance, particularly of sidewalks along the "structurals," is less than satisfactory. The "24-hour street," along which stores had to be open all but one hour each day to cater to night-life (or insomniacs), may not have been the best idea in the world. The "rurban villages" are not celebrated. By the late 1990s the downtown area was losing some of its appeal, particularly in the evenings, as other destinations developed and as older movie theaters were replaced with multiplexes in shopping malls not too far from the center. By 2009, the 300-person buses were starting to look and sound a bit the worse for wear. They could certainly do with a respray to restore them to their original Ferrari red.

Curitiba is not without its nay-sayers. Some people are keen to focus on the errors, and on the projects and programs that didn't work or were ill conceived. Socio-economic non-programs are a special target. To this observer, though, much of the criticism seems to come from professional doubters and real or would-be academicians, not unlike those Ph.D. students and professors to be found at Berkeley's Department of City and Regional Planning. No matter. There has been so much international recognition, and indeed duplication, of Curitiba's achievements that they are more than able to speak for themselves.

Two substantive threads run through the whole Curitiba project: the subjects of the government-led efforts; and the mindsets and natures of the people most closely involved. Both speak of the transferability of ideas and programs to other communities. Subject-wise, the Curitiba effort started with a simple, understandable, physical plan for the city – call it a framework plan – that was tied to social and economic objectives. If the idea of a plan is not transferable, then urban planners have no reason to exist. Central to their plan was the idea of a high-capacity mass-transit system tied to very straightforward and dense land-use locations. A major emphasis on large parks and open spaces, both for themselves and as urban form-givers, was central to the notion of what a good city should be: make those improvements while you still can. Open space is harder to achieve as land becomes more expensive and vested interests become set.

Environmental responsibility via a host of mandatory and voluntary educational programs is now commonplace the world over. Curitiba holds no patent on this notion. However, it did start early, and proceeded with some panache. The Free University of the Environment; the practical memorial honoring the memory of Chico Mendez; trading bus tickets for environmental clean-up efforts. These and other eminently transferable projects were pursued with showmanship and a smile. Rolling a long piece of paper down the center of Main Street every Saturday morning and handing out paint and brushes to kids, both rich and poor, who might like to paint, and might have parents in tow, who in turn might talk to each other while their kids paint, and might thereby develop a better sense and feeling about something called community, may not be directly transferable from one city to another, but certainly the spirit of doing simple, community-making things is.

Doing projects and programs that you can afford, and inventing things that you can afford, is – or ought to be – a transferable lesson from Curitiba. It is a lesson that is extremely important for U.S. cities. A rail rapid-transit system, on or below ground, might have been speedier and probably more elegant than Curitiba's articulated buses. But there was no way that such a system was affordable, and it would have taken years to implement. So, instead, the city devised its own system – including the invention of the boarding tubes – to fit its own public purse. And, it did it all with speed. The schools and libraries are all of a piece, concerned with getting things done quickly for the people, not building architectural showpieces. The streetlights and early bus shelters were all erected fast and on the cheap. These people were not dummies. They knew that some of their projects would not last; that time would take its toll on them. They also anticipated that their economic means would grow over time. So if something had proved a success, its replacement could be of higher quality and better design. If, on the other hand, something had been a failure, it was easy to forget it; after all, not much money had been wasted on it in the first place. In the U.S. we do things expensively: costly materials, costly signature designs, costly programs. So we do one or two streets or segments, one park, always less than is needed, with the notion (or self-deception) that we will do more later. But we do not.

How to characterize the people most closely involved in Curitiba's vast improvements and their mindsets? And what is to be taken from them that might be helpful to other city builders? This is in part an issue of leadership and commitment and stubbornness that will continue to be important. These were and are people with noble ideas and ideals of which they are not ashamed. They treasure and honor creativity. They are public entrepreneurs, always with the city and its people uppermost in their minds. In short, theirs has been a positive outlook, a "we can do it" approach to city building. Their humor has also been extremely important.

The members of the Curitiba group are extraordinarily self-reliant in outlook and approach to making proposals real. They will accept help whenever it is offered but will never depend on someone else, some larger government. If no help is forthcoming, they will figure out how to achieve what they want. They may have big ideas but they understand incrementalism, with a "make each day better than the previous one" mentality. They are prepared to begin undertakings even when they don't have all the answers. And there has seemed to be little fear of failure, combined with a cautious use of outside experts, particularly in the traffic-planning field, often wedded to textbook formulas and computer models that, in the end, discourage innovation. As might be expected, there has been no great reliance on legislation to achieve plans. These people have been effective and have been given responsibility and power because they have built and maintained trust. There is honesty in what they do.

The Curitibanos who have achieved so much did not get up every morning with a world view. They did not get out of their beds reminding themselves that they lived in a developing country with thoughts of limited resources and therefore limited options. Rather, they observed problems and opportunities, then got on with the job of solving the problems, exploiting the opportunities, and building a better community. It is worthwhile, I think, to remember a favorite saying of Jaime Lerner: "Tendency is not destiny."

Part VI

World-Class Cities

Memos on Pudong

Memo one: What is world class?

I warned you about prattling on to the Shanghai people and to your central area government colleagues in Beijing about your term "World-Class City" for the Pudong area, across the river from Shanghai. Now they tell you they've decided to do it, to build Pudong, but they want you to tell them, first, what a world-class city is. Remember, you promised them a world-class city, not me. Are you sure they're not just pulling your leg when they ask, "What is a world-class city?" But I guess you had better say something.

Maybe an easy way out would be to say that what you meant, simply, is a really well-planned, large community that works well functionally, economically, and socially, one that is recognized as having grace and beauty, and one which is able to adapt, over the years, to changing times, all while being respectful of the land on which it is located. But I suspect you want more, so here are some thoughts that might be useful for you. Let me know what you think.

A world-class city might be one which has characteristics so outstanding as compared to other cities that the particular city is looked to as the epitome of those qualities, or one of the very few that has them; something to strive toward if that is what you want. A world-class athlete is someone who has reached a supremely high level of performance – that is, the very top group – at or near the record in whatever it is that she does. Of course, a world-class athlete is rarely world class in more than one sport or even one event or position, so that implies specialization. Actually some cities are like that, noted for one attribute, but maybe you didn't mean that.

Sometimes, people refer to "world class" in relation to size or amount of activity, especially economic activity. I hope you mean more than that. Quality of an attribute may be as important as quantity. I would hope, in Pudong, that we will be talking about quality more than quantity. Florence is not very large. Would you call Florence a world-class city? In the world of art one would surely call it that. Of course, there was a time when Florence was more renowned for cloth and political power. It would be generally agreed that the Piazza del Campo in Siena, the Piazza Navona in Rome, and the series of spaces in the Forbidden City in Beijing are all world-class places.

There must be bridges that are world class and engineers who design them who are world class. I would imagine that a world-class bridge would be one that is or was exceptionally innovative in design, something new and appropriate to the situation that is later used as a model of a type for other bridges; or it might possess a special grace (agreed to as such by many); or exhibit a new or daring structural approach to a problem. New cities could have such attributes, too. I suspect that a new world-class city, one that I might be prepared to label as such, would use a minimum of scarce resources, and would be environmentally friendly, known to be so. Isn't that a huge challenge for our age?

Some cities are world class because of their size. Mexico City or Tokyo or New York or Singapore might be examples. They are in that growing group of economic centers or national capitals that seem to compete for being the biggest in the world. It is bigness and the concentration of power (often economic but perhaps political as well, like Washington) that can impact the world and accounts for their importance. Often it is the attributes that come with bigness that enhance the image of "world class" – art and culture in New York, for example.

Does tangible evidence of history make a city world class? If so, then Rome would surely be world class. But would Athens? Or Istanbul? Setting and uniqueness, a physical structure appropriate to the setting, must have something to do with specialness, if not world classness. Rio has it; São Paulo, where the money is, does not. What would San Francisco be without its setting? Not as important a place!

Aside from bigness and economic power, I'm not sure why Tokyo would be considered world class. There are some wonderful streets in Tokyo – Omote Sando and the short residential street in Setagaya – but overall I think it's the bigness, the economic power, and the bustle that most characterize the city. Mexico City has some world-class pieces – the Reforma, the anthropological museum, the subway system – but aside from its bigness, would you call it world class? In addition to numbers of people, the concentration of economic power, and its art, music and drama, New York's world classness comes from its physical bigness, the huge number of tall, tall buildings grouped very close together.

Paris, for sure, is a world-class city. It has to do, I think, with bigness, history, art, culture, civic beauty constantly maintained, design, style, intellectual ferment, physical grace, oneness in the public realm and, perhaps, in ways that I cannot explain, an insistence on the importance of the French language. If

Sydney is a world-class city, it would be because of the Opera House alone. Hong Kong? Why? Setting? Size? All that activity and energy?

If I were designing a city from scratch, I'd be concerned with health, physical comfort, public life, compactness – qualities that might help people achieve together what they could not achieve singly. Graciousness, diversity, and a complementary relationship with the land and natural environment would be central. I'd be more concerned with quality than with quantity, but I would not equate high quality with high cost. One could do worse than just set down a memorable street pattern, transportation system, and open-space plan.

My understanding is that Shanghai has been able to sustain itself, in terms of food production, for many years. That is truly remarkable. Much of the inhabitants' food, I gather, is grown in the Pudong area, within an overnight trip to the city. In the future, a real world-class city, one that others might well try to emulate, would be a city that integrated agriculture and all food and energy production into and along with the whole urban fabric in a mutually supportive way to create a self-sustaining metropolis. You might want to suggest this idea to the biggies that you're dealing with.

Memo two: Planning world class in Pudong

I'm glad I got to see Shanghai and Pudong. The Pudong countryside is indeed impressive. I didn't expect to see, so close to Shanghai, just across the river, so much open and attractive agricultural land; little or no urban sprawl here, I guess. Nor had I been led to expect all the water courses, large and small, that are there, very complicated.

Jaime and I took the opportunity of meeting with local people to suggest our alternative development approach to the one we had seen, the one that has development taking place seemingly all over Pudong, with large spaces between very tall buildings. Our ideas, you will recall, envision a tight, linear band of development along the river across from Shanghai, about one mile wide, served by a central transit line that would be easily accessible. For reasons of scarce resources, including steel and electricity, most development would be low, but very dense, with easy access to the river, along which would be a lineal park. An intent was to save as much land as possible in its natural state and for food production. We expressed to local planners and officials that there were other approaches than the ones they were pursuing, and that they could save and use most of the land for other purposes, food mostly, and still have what they wanted with well over a million people accommodated. We showed how much land our approach would require, as opposed to the sprawl we've seen proposed.

The response to Jaime and me and our ideas was cordial, but it is very clear that they will have none of it. Singapore is the model they have in mind: big, big buildings all over the place, even taller than those in Singapore, and use all the land you want. I could tell that they were just putting up with us, being civil. Clearly, my idea of what might be a great city is not what the planners of Pudong want. Nor do they share concerns about going lightly on the land, developing only what is necessary, minimizing travel space, and maximizing land to remain in food production and in water sources.

By the way, you never responded to my memo on what makes a great city, nor to the material I sent to you on density. Nor have you responded to our ideas about how best to develop Pudong. Increasingly, I get the sense that Singapore and Hong Kong are your models, too. So, why are we associated on this endeavor? Why don't we call it quits? I am grateful to you for giving me the opportunity to see Shanghai. I learned a great deal walking around the city. Clearly, they are intent on clearing away all the old, tight housing areas where poor people live, building new, block-like projects for the displaced, on the out-skirts, and rebuilding the old areas for luxury hotels, offices, and expensive housing. It's not very different than what American cities did in the fifties, sixties, and seventies. It has its own boredom.

Memo three: Building has started

I don't know where you are, but wherever you are, I thought you'd want to be brought up to speed on Pudong. A lot of it is now built and there's much more to come.

It's very big; very big, tall, tall buildings, with more in the works. Buildings have significant distances between them, at least for now. Roads are large and so are blocks. The overall layout is much more consistent with a driving than a walking environment. They're using a lot of land and they plan to use more. In other words, forget or be prepared to forget food production as a high priority. And they might figure that water and draining matters can be worked around or solved as needed.

On the "mainland," in Shanghai, they have been doing more of what they had started. It isn't exactly like Singapore, for sure, but it's the same model. Funny, isn't it, that at one point the Singapore people came to realize that they'd better stop producing travel posters with small-scale chop houses seen behind an array of small, colorful fishing boats: they realized that they had torn down most of those buildings and that the fishing boats were no longer there. False advertising! It may have been then that they began to realize that history and old buildings might be important and might even have some value. And Orchard Road, with its line-up of shopping malls, might not be the fine street it once was, especially as a place to walk, and they began to find ways of changing it. One might argue that Pudong, too, can change, if they want it to, or see the need. But why build it the way they have to start?

And what about all that productive agricultural land? China is on an economic roll now, early in the 21st century. Food may not seem an urgent issue these days, especially with all the new technology geared to high productivity.

(Hey, forget that in the long run that stuff may well do more harm than good and that population control by choice is a lot better than starving and killing – we'll deal with that later.) But it's not so long ago that China had very real food problems; it may still and just keeps them out of sight. And – who knows? – they could have them again. Agricultural land, once gone, is and will be hard to get back. The better that land is, the more is the pity.

I think you'd like what they're doing in Pudong. You'd find answers to my criticisms and, like a Mayor of San Francisco said long ago, when he decided to embrace the double-decked Embarcadero Freeway, "It may be ugly, but we can't stop progress." You'd be for the bold and the new. Sometimes, though, what seems to be progress isn't progress. So, wherever you are – from above or below, or sideways – take a look at Pudong. I wonder if you think it's a world-class city in the making.

Part VII

City Certainties

Parking

Traffic is Not a Problem

Cities that are obsessed with the movement of cars and spend a lot of time and money trying to avoid or solve traffic problems are invariably less livable than cities that don't.

The traffic in Rome is really screwed up and it doesn't seem that the Romans spend a lot of time trying to solve the problems. Certainly they don't widen streets or build new bridges or freeways or anything like that. It's a terrific city. In an hour a stranger knows that he's perfectly safe on the streets. You just walk wherever you want to walk, purposefully, directly, being careful not to pay attention to the cars, and you know you'll be perfectly safe. They'll miss you. But don't confuse them by trying to guess what they're going to do because they don't know what you might do and you could be hit.

The drivers know about traffic jams. They know the rules will change daily as to where they can and cannot go; they find new ways to get to places, ways that work for about two days. They complain a lot. They adjust. Everyone adjusts. They know that there's no real way to solve the problem unless you want to do so at the expense of something really important, less countable than traffic, like, say, the Coliseum, or the Piazza Navona. So they adjust. Mussolini, I'm told, wanted to put a road through the Piazza Navona, and look what happened to him.

Life takes place on the streets and in the piazzas and it's possible to talk over an espresso at the bar about the rotten traffic mess and how it's getting worse. The traffic jams make it livable. People get where they're going, roughly on time. What else do you want?

The French worry a bit more about traffic than the Italians. They still have pretensions of world power and leadership and associate that with being up to date. So Paris, though a really classy city, isn't as full of life as Rome. They'd have done better not to have screwed up part of the Seine with that speedway.

San Francisco, where they stopped building freeways in the nick of time, is more livable than Los Angeles. They worry like crazy about moving cars in Los Angeles, and they spend a lot of money to do just that. What has it got them? More problems. Cleveland was once a real city until they spent money on traffic instead of on the city. There are freeways all over San Diego and they widen streets at the first sign of a traffic jam. I've never seen such wide streets. The sidewalks are narrow. Every person I've ever met there has one of those Thomas Map guides because they'd be lost without one. Now, electronic maps are doing the job. They spend their time figuring out where the street is that they want to get to and how to get from here to there, instead of actually being wherever "there" is. Phoenix has lots of roads but it's not a city any more. It's a developed area. Gertrude Stein was wrong, there is a "there" in Oakland. It's Phoenix that has no "there."

The guys who call themselves real thinkers on this subject admit privately (and maybe in small seminars where regular people aren't allowed) that traffic congestion cannot be solved. It's like parking. So they talk about management.

One Sunday, I was driving on a freeway outside of Rome and there was clearly too much traffic for the two lanes painted on the concrete. All of a sudden there were three lanes, then four. People turned a two-lane highway into a four-lane highway until the traffic thinned out. They adapted. In Los Angeles they would have widened the freeway and it would still be jammed.

How come, whenever I find a city or a street where the traffic works – like in Rome, or along those really nice boulevards in Paris, like Avenue Montaigne, where it's tough to figure out how things work at an intersection, or on the narrow streets of downtown Philadelphia, or up the really steep streets in San Francisco – some traffic engineer tells me it doesn't work and that their fraternity would never approve something similar these days?

If you're into worrying, then, it's okay to worry about traffic. But just don't do anything about it or you'll make where you live worse. Better yet, come to understand that traffic isn't a problem and you'll see, your city will be better.

Parking is Not a Problem

If you frequently go to a very crowded, congested area, you always find a parking space, and usually with ease. If you seldom go to that same area, you will rarely succeed in finding a space.

This truth was revealed to me in the North Beach section of San Francisco. I used to go there often – to have coffee, to meet friends, to shop at the Florence Ravioli Company, now sadly gone, to eat at Tomasso's, the North Beach Restaurant, the Washington Square Bar and Grille, some other eateries no longer there, and just to walk around. North Beach is a crowded area and there aren't many places to park if you have to get there by car. But that never stopped me driving there and I always found a spot. If I were meeting someone, I'd rarely be more than five minutes late.

Then I left the city for about four months. When I returned, I couldn't find a place to park in North Beach and I was damned if I'd use the public garage on Vallejo Street; a matter of pride. At first I concluded that more people must be driving there; more cars and fewer places. But it wasn't long, maybe a week or two, before I started finding parking spaces again with ease. Even today it's no problem.

When I go to the symphony at the Civic Center, I plan to arrive outside about five minutes before it starts. I know I'll find a place to park, even if there's an opera across the street that night and a recital up the block, at Herbst Hall. There are four particular spots and I know that at least one of them will be vacant, waiting for me. There are others, too – a bit more chancy, but often free. Sure, just a few of these spaces have colors painted along the curb: a red here, a yellow or a green there, sometimes a white. I have never known what any of them mean. Some have the letters S.F.P.D. on them. I figure that must mean "Saved for Planning Director," and I was once one of those. In any case, ticket-givers in any sane city[1] don't give tickets at all the possible places, and it's only a matter of time before you understand where and when they do and don't. Nevertheless, most of the places where I park are unpainted. Recently, I bought a Smart car, which is really short. In San Francisco, with its never-ending curb cuts for driveways leading to unsightly garages, there is rarely enough space to park a standard or even a modest car. But there's plenty of room for my car.

So what does this mean? Regarding parking, if you want or need to go somewhere, you find a way, you adjust; everybody adjusts; even the system adjusts. Which means that paying a lot of attention to parking is a waste of time and energy. It's one of those problems that takes care of itself. If you don't pay attention to it, it goes away; and that's the best thing to do because if you think too much about it, it's unsolvable, even with all the pricey mechanisms now in vogue; and places with lots of parking are usually lousy places to go anyway. If absolutely no parking exists at a place you'd like to be, you'll find another way to get there. What sane person even thinks of driving to downtown San Francisco, or Manhattan? On the other hand, there is a lot of room to park in the desert or in the asphalt around most shopping malls. There is not much in North Beach, and there are a lot of people there. So don't worry about parking. It's really not a problem.

Note

1   Berkeley, California, does not fit into any category. There, they have at least one parking patrol person for every two parking spaces, and that's reason enough not to want to live there. Bureaucratic lightheartedness is hard to find in Berkeley, either in the city or at the university.

Things Can Get Better or Worse

I've noticed that no matter how bad things are, they can get worse. And often they do. It's like that with cities, too. The city is broke, but then it gets more broke. As if to give credibility to the rumor that he liked to trash fine urban communities, Phillip Johnson couldn't have designed anything worse than the blank-walled, harlequin Neiman Marcus Building at Union Square in San Francisco – almost no windows, lots of blank walls with diamond shapes. But then he or his firm designed the strange circular office tower at the foot of California Street, where it meets Market Street. It's worse, with no relationship to the street and repelling open space. It's hard to do that. Attacks on our sensibilities are without end. Things can always get worse. Consider San Francisco's new Federal Office Building, an immense, hulking, bulky growth, totally out of scale with the city.

On the other hand, no matter how good things are, they can always get better. Even if we're really satisfied today, tomorrow we can think of a way to be more satisfied. If it's a great neighborhood, let's make it better. Having the Golden Gate Park is really good, but the Golden Gate National Recreation Area makes things even better. Some tourists and the things that attract them are fine. Maybe more would be better. Crissy Field makes San Francisco much better than it was without it.

Of course, at some point you can have too much of a good thing. It's hard to believe that Fisherman's Wharf was once real, with real fishing boats and fish processing that people came to see and enjoy. A cable-car line started and ended there. There is very little left that has to do with fishing. Cry for Florence, which simply cannot cope with all the tourists and remain Florence. The same goes for Venice. On the other hand, in some places traffic congestion is so bad that the streets become nice places to walk again. "Pray for gridlock!" can be a serious exhortation.

So, things can always get better or worse.

What You Believe Counts

If you believe that you must build on small pieces of land, and if you believe that buildings must be built under a certain height, then it will be economic to do that. If you do not believe that you are limited to small parcels or limited height, or other limitations, then it won't be economic. The key word is "believe," and that's a lot of what land economics is all about.

For longer than I care to remember, developers, their architects, and people who call themselves "land economists" have been telling me that in order to build efficiently and economically it is necessary to have large parcels of land so that large and presumably efficient floors can be built in their buildings. Height, I am told, is necessary mostly to get enough space in the buildings to pay for the costs of land and because big corporations want to be in big buildings. It has to do with economics and efficiency rates and things "penciling out" and images.

When I found myself in Tokyo, in its most intensely built-up central shopping district, I saw a lot of buildings, many of them new, on small lots, as narrow as 25 feet wide, some even narrower. They were often ten storeys high, which is certainly modest by today's standards. I saw apartment buildings, offices, hotels, even a department store, none of them terribly high, all on those small, small lots. So, why did the Japanese build that way? Did they know nothing of economics? Maybe, I thought, all those small parcels were separately owned and no one would give them up because having land was really important, and the government hadn't yet figured out a way to assemble all the small pieces (and maybe all the small owners) into large parcels (for a few large owners). And maybe there were tough height laws that were unlikely to be changed. Later, in other areas, I saw new large buildings that were a lot higher than ten storeys on large parcels. In any case, there remained all those modest-scaled buildings. I think it was just that the Japanese in that area knew that there were unbendable limits to what was allowed, so they lived within the limits and everything, including economics, adjusted to what was perceived as real. The areas with the smaller buildings – with their separate entrances and signs and all of the diversity that is possible with more buildings rather than fewer – were much more interesting than those with the large buildings. In fact, the latter were pretty dull.

Washington has always managed to live with very strict height limits. No one seriously believes the height limits can be changed. Prices and economics and land uses have adjusted. Sure, developers do all kinds of things just outside Washington. They build some pretty terrible stuff. But if the governments outside Washington said, "No way, you must build under eight storeys," or whatever, you know they'd find a way to do that. But wouldn't that mean that more land would have to be developed and there would be more sprawl into the countryside? Maybe; maybe not. Those areas of tall, large buildings are often characterized by large open spaces between the towers, open spaces covered with wide streets and acres of auto parking. No one walks between those buildings because they're too far apart. Low land coverage is not necessarily a big deal. They could build lower and cover more of the properties and not spread out so much.

A major developer in Boston, a very successful one, once said to me, "You know what it is, don't you? It's expectations." He could have said, "It's greed." As recently as April 2010, in San Francisco, a developer's proposal for a 400-foot-plus building in an area with a 200-foot height limit was about to be denied. Objections from Russian Hill, Telegraph Hill, and North Beach activists were persuasive. At the last minute, seeing the handwriting on the wall, the developer agreed not to exceed the limit. Why had he proposed the larger building in the first place? Why was it suddenly economic to build within the law? Might "Let's see what I can get away with" have had anything to do with the larger proposal?

It's simple. If there's a rule or a norm or a habit that says that the most you can do with a piece of land is such-and-such and everyone really believes that rule and that it cannot or should not be changed, then people and prices adjust, and that's that. If, on the other hand, people think they can get more out of or on to the land, by a rule change or some special consideration that others don't have, and make more money in the doing, then they will scream bloody murder that it's uneconomic to develop under the rules. Worse yet, some of them even come to believe it and develop big economic theories about it. And the ultimate threat is that if the rules are not changed or bent to let the developers do what they "need" to do, they'll go somewhere else. People get scared and believe them and change the rules.

But I'll tell you, if they believed they *had to* build on small lots and only to a certain height, it would be economic.

Part VIII

San Francisco

Golden Gate Bridge

Reflecting on San Francisco

"Location! Location! Location!" say the retail marketing gurus of the three most important determinants of worldly success. Cities are not retail outlets but location may well be the key factor in how well they progress, and in this San Francisco is truly a privileged city. Small by American standards – just 45 square miles; Los Angeles has about ten times that area – at the tip of a long peninsula, surrounded by water on three sides and hills to the south, San Francisco enjoys a commanding entrance to a magnificent protected bay that in turn gives access, far inland, to the north, south, and east, to a remarkably fertile hinterland and, in the mid-1800s, to the most precious of metals at the foothills of the Sierra range. The climate is salubrious (though spoiled natives would hardly agree), and there are hills, lots of hills, that afford splendid vistas in every direction. North and south of the city is the magnificent redwood coastal range of giant trees, a spectacular, rot-and-insect-defying, adaptive building material if ever there was one. Oakland, across the bay, makes a better location for the terminus of transcontinental rail travel, but San Francisco would find ways to accommodate that problem. All in all, it is a wonderful place to locate a city. It is a city of wonderful and historically valued views, to and from the hills, to and from water, and to the East Bay.

By 1967 the city was largely developed. Street grids had long since been platted and built, famously without regard to topography, land had been sub-divided into many small parcels, sold and in some cases built upon again. The earthquake and fire of 1906 devastated large parts of downtown and its imme-diate surrounds. Soon to be as celebrated as it was mourned, the earthquake proved to be only a temporary setback in the city's development. The large areas left vacant by the fire were, for the most part, rebuilt following pre-event patterns and forms. And that has been the general rule after major fire disasters in other U.S. cities, too, rather than taking advantage of the re-platting opportunities and rebuilding on a larger scale. There was no shortage of grand plans, but it was easier to return to established patterns, largely determined by land-ownership. Indeed, that has most often been the lesson to be learned from abrupt, large, natural disasters, at least until Hurricane Katrina in 2005: that people, being ornery, rebuild largely in ways that previously existed.

Be that as it may, if San Francisco were largely developed by 1967, the year I arrived to be its planning director, what was there left to plan? What was the challenge in this physically small, dense city? To be sure, there were large undeveloped or underused areas along the eastern shoreline, mostly associated with shipping and industry, but these were not the challenge of the moment. The challenge was change: not the change that might come as a result of earthquake or fire, but that brought on by the constancy of economically driven physical development. San Francisco, like so many American cities, was changing in significant ways. Ironically, what nature had not done, man was intent on doing. To address real or imagined urban problems – of physical deterioration, of unsafe and unsanitary housing conditions, of circulation problems and inadequate public infrastructures, of poor people living in housing thought to be substandard – the federal government, urged on by the best intentions of fine, socially responsible people, had embarked in the late 1940s on a major, nationwide program of publicly subsidized urban redevelopment. There were large federal subsidies available to cities that permitted public land-taking and clearance of large deteriorated areas after replanning them. The program made some sense in older Eastern and Midwestern cities; not so much sense in San Francisco. Not to be denied its share of federal largess, San Francisco's policy-makers had convinced themselves of the city's deterioration and had embarked on large-scale land and people clearance projects and dreams of sparkling new urban environments. Data that showed relatively few of the structures in the Western Addition to be seriously deteriorated were never made public by the Redevelopment Agency. Much of the housing was built of first-cut virgin redwood; very solid stuff.

The federal highway program was also bringing change in the form of freeways (I was uninformed about the freeway revolt that had taken place in the city in 1966, to bring a halt to that kind of change). The already completed San Francisco freeways may have dislocated more people than federally sponsored redevelopment and there had been plans to build many more.

Purely private development initiatives didn't happen all in one place or at one time but they were constant, and were changing the face of San Francisco. Most were greeted with civic silence and some, such as the Bank of America Building, public commendation. But the Fontana Towers, two slab residential high rises along the northern waterfront, were more than visible amid their small-scale context, blocking views of the bay that people cherished and took for granted, and so caused an angry response. Change was surely happening, but I knew little of these matters when I was first informed about the job opening in early 1967.

Change was part of what attracted me to San Francisco as a place to work. Attending a city planning conference in the early 1960s, I did what tourists were expected to do: took a trip to the "Top of the Mark" Hopkins Hotel on Nob Hill to have a drink and admire the view. Spectacular! Like no other city I had experienced. And yet, looking west and north, new intrusions were clearly visible, and some weren't all that nice. Did people realize that filling in, between the hills, with new, tall buildings might not be the best thing to do? Nor was a walk along the waterfront, to Fisherman's Wharf, a particularly pleasant way to spend time. Where was the bay? Where might one walk in comfort?

Personal change was more important as a reason to try my hand in San Francisco. I felt I had finished my "apprenticeship" after one year as a city planner–designer in Cleveland, another eight years of intense work in Pittsburgh, and two years in Calcutta. I had returned from India to a teaching role at the University of Pennsylvania. I was welcomed but was not entirely comfortable with academia, particularly at a time of erupting black anger and "long hot summers," to say nothing of growing civil discontent with the Vietnam War. I didn't share the same vocabulary with many of my university colleagues. The language they used to explain urban phenomena was often foreign to my ways of thinking and expression. Times were changing and it was a time to be working in the field. Doing rather than talking was important to me, and perhaps I wanted to make my mark. Arrogance? Quite probably. And there was San Francisco, a one-of-a-kind, beautiful city, wonderfully set, and it was looking for a director of city planning. Why not?

Naivety and some ignorance can go a long way in helping a person get going in a new job. Vastly different than local governments I had been accustomed to in Cleveland, Pittsburgh, and Philadelphia, San Francisco's in 1967 was basically a no-power-to-anyone form of government: a mix of a commission form (there were then 22 of them, including the City Planning Commission) and a modified city manager (called Chief Administrative Officer), under whom were seven key operating departments, such as public works and public health. The Chief Administrative Officer was appointed for life, could not be fired, and so was the most powerful person in government, more so in the day-to-day operations of the city than the Mayor or the 11 elected city council members, known as the supervisors. The major player in city development was the Redevelopment Agency, very well funded via federal programs, and free of the staff-hiring constraints imposed by the city's very rigid civil service system. Put simply, the agency, run by its very politically astute director, Justin Herman, could and did run roughshod over the Planning Department on large land development projects involving physical change. The Recreation and Parks Department was pretty much a fiefdom of its own, as was the Department of Public Works on matters of streets and traffic, with special fondness for street widening and one-way streets.

The Planning Department had going for it a mandate to prepare a Master Plan for the city, a what-should-go-where document, and responsibility for zoning (public controls over the uses of private land), as well as a requirement that proposed public undertakings involving roadways, traffic, and uses of public land be referred to it for findings – not approval or denial – as to conformity to the Master Plan. There were other mandates but those were the most outstanding. The Mayor, John Shelley, was in the third year of his first (and last) term, having previously been in the U.S. Congress for many years. Jack Kent, once the city's planning director and the founder of the University of California's city planning program, but by then in the Mayor's office, advised me that turnover of a planning director with a change in Mayor was not expected, and I took him at his word.

The supervisors, I soon found, were largely conservative and seemed not to have city planning on their minds. One, William Blake, repeatedly called everyone's attention to the fact that the city had paid my moving expenses from the East and suggested that it should pay to send me back. He also reminded everyone in earshot that via the Planning Department they had spent a small fortune on a housing study, a predictive model run by academics at Berkeley, which didn't work. Blake was keen to know what new wonderfulness I might bring to the city.

With supreme naivety, soon after arriving, I succumbed to a young man's pleading not to state my reasons for terminating his six-month probationary employment period as it might hurt his chances of getting a job elsewhere. (He had proved to be incompetent.) He then appealed against the decision, pointing out to the Civil Service Commission that I had neglected to give reasons for his termination. Backed by his union, he was ordered back to me as a permanent, never-to-be-fired staff member.

True, I had not looked into these and many other matters before deciding to move to San Francisco. Perhaps, at the time, I felt it was so important to try my hand at being the head planner of a dense, storeyed city in a very troubled social period that I wasn't open to looking seriously at the limitations of the job.

On reflection, in regards to city planning, the particular organizational form of local government, though important, may be less so than I once thought. One isn't likely to find, in any form of government, many mayors who might be characterized as "planners' mayors." The long run is not normally their focus, nor is comprehensiveness (how does one thing impact another?), nor the quality of what gets built. They tend to be more concerned with solving immediate problems, with projects, and with leaving legacies. They are pummeled constantly by movers and shakers, and don't care to hear about setting bad precedents. They are too intelligent to aspire to complex utopian dreams. John Shelley, after a long career in Congress, was not terribly active; and Joe Alioto was very much a pragmatist. Of the next six mayors, only Art Agnos could be termed a person who was highly concerned with planning. And he lasted just one term. There are few truly visionary and city-loving mayors: Joe Riley of Charleston and Jaime Lerner of Curitiba are rarities. City council members may be somewhat more concerned with planning issues than are mayors, particularly with regard to their districts if they are elected by geographical subdivisions. But even if local governmental structures and processes are oriented to physical plans and designs and actions consistent with them, there are few assurances that they will be regularly followed. Other departments beyond planning have their own mandates, power, and other interests. There are priorities other than those of city planning in a city: the what should go where, why, how, and when.

Being effective may, in the end, be determined as much or more by the people doing the planning, the particular set of actors involved, the activism or apathy of the citizenry, and the times than by one or another organizational chart. It is people who make things tick, or not. Strongly advocated, highly competent, and imaginative professional work has a way of being recognized and appreciated, and I think we achieved that in San Francisco. Certainly we tried.

Naivety and some ignorance, then, may not have been such terrible traits as I started in San Francisco. At least they allowed me to enter the ball game. Sure, I may soon have said, "My God, had I known that, I never would have come." But by then, it was too late. So, you do your best.

No one plans or replans a city alone; it takes a lot of people. Despite an arcane civil service system geared to achieving and maintaining at best a mediocre staff, there were some absolutely first-rate people in the department in 1967, when I arrived.

Peter Svirsky, a soft-spoken land-use attorney, was there. Put simply, he was brilliant, no one fooled with him, and he was extremely influential over the long run. Somehow, he could walk out of a meeting with billboard company representatives with the amortization schedules for their San Francisco billboards. We could then write an ordinance geared to a timed removal of same and, surprise, surprise, when challenged by one of their people as to the short time periods we set, could produce their data as rationale for what we were proposing. The city attorney's office regularly deferred to Peter on land-use and zoning questions. He could also write clearly, in language that would hold up legally at the same time as laypeople could understand and even be inspired by it.

Jim Paul and Jim White were recently out of school, perhaps an early contingent of the bright, energetic, happy, devil-may-care people then flocking to the city. Paul, an urban sociologist, had a way of being welcomed and accepted by everyone, at the same time as he was a fine and firm analyst of housing data and people's ability to pay for shelter. White, an architect, was a fine budding urban designer. Beyond their abilities, they brought lighthearted joy to the office. Tom Malloy was another. Some of the older, able people had been beaten by abuse and time. Sammy Jung, who in his early years had a perfectly viable idea of how to deal physically with what was to become the Embarcadero Freeway – bury it, at least in front of the Ferry Building – had been derided publicly, I was told. It took some doing to get him to open up and contribute, but in time he did, bringing a very detailed knowledge of the city to the table. Phoebe

Brown, related to the Hearst family and thereby a San Francisco "blue blood," was older than most, very patrician in demeanor. She was in charge of a neighborhood plan being done for the largely black and low-income South Bayshore area. Soon I, too, was very much involved in its planning. Two old-time drafting staff were quite able not only as cartographers but as researchers and graphic designers. I had to prove myself worthy of their skills before they would let them be seen. A problem was that none or precious few of these people, old or new, had been trained or had done any city planning or urban design.

Unfortunately, on the flip side of the few good people were many more, some in senior positions, who were not particularly able or, for whatever reason, had long since stopped working very hard. What to do about them? Feeling that nothing good was likely to come from them, one strategy was simply to ignore them. To some extent, that is what I did, soon tiring of giving research lessons as well as paragraph-structure direction to staff who might never learn. Perhaps more creatively, on grounds of efficiency, I chose to assign work to the most junior people who were capable of doing a job, with the upshot that some senior staff found themselves working for their juniors.

It wasn't difficult to attract bright, young, capable people to seek employment with us, however unattractive the reputation of the department. Word gets out quickly that one is serious about doing socially relevant, high-quality work, and applicants come seeking a chance to be part of a good thing. Dennis and Trixie Ryan were two of them. Of course, the romance of being in San Francisco helped. Those were the flower-children, hippie, "summer of love" days. Hiring the best of the applicants, however, was no easy trick. Ever fearful and unknowing of the statute of limitations regarding breaking civil service regulations to hire staff, and perhaps a bit ashamed of some of the things I did to get them, even to this day, it must suffice to say that I ended up with a lot of "temporary" staff – temporary for three to five years. Bruce Anderson – who joined me after graduating from the University of Pennsylvania – or I interviewed every person who came our way looking for a job. If they were good, and if we could find a way, however sneaky, to get them on to the staff, we would. Emily Hill was such a person. Failing that, we would advise them of job opportunities in the area. In short, we ran an employment agency. Young people remember that kind of help and will help you, in turn, if they can. Regularly, we, the staff, mixed our professional and social lives; that, too, proved to be beneficial in getting and keeping a first-rate staff. By the time two years had gone by, I could boast of what I considered to be as good a public staff as could be found anywhere.

The turn-of-the-century Burnham Plan for Chicago is long remembered and referenced, at least in city development circles. Talk with Chicago's elected officials, with city planners, with architects, or with local aficionados and, sooner or later, you are likely to hear about that plan and how it remains a major force in how the city develops. And yet, whenever I have had reason to compare what the city has actually done with what that plan advocated, adherence to it has seemed to be as much in the breach as in the following. There have been other well-known plans for American cities – for Philadelphia, for Savannah (perhaps the most memorable), for Washington, D.C., New York, Detroit, and Portland, to name but a few. But for most of them the memorability usually rests with the physical structure first established on the ground – the streets, blocks, and major open spaces or networks, the initial form-givers – rather than with subsequent citywide plans. In North America, the locally much-remembered and often cited Bartholomew plan for Vancouver, of the late 1920s, is an exception. Vancouverites still pay attention to it. What of the citywide, long-range plans for San Francisco? What becomes of them?

If for no other reason than to stave off embarrassment, the operative San Francisco Master Plan had to be redone in 1967. Its call for freeways, rejected by elected officials and citizens alike, would have been a tragedy if even a part of it were to be achieved. The rest was a dull, mimeographed document that could be interpreted in many ways and would inspire no one. But there was no money to take on the preparation of a new citywide plan, and no demand for it either. Nor was I enamored by the prospect. More immediate matters of looming projects, necessary responses to individual building proposals, two neighborhood plans, citywide housing issues, and internal staffing problems demanded attention. What, though, was to be the basis for all the day-to-day physical development decisions, to say nothing of the neighborhood and district or city-impacting recommendations that are required, such as whether there should be a new bridge across the bay? You could not "wing it" for ever. Without funds to undertake a grand effort, a revision of the city plan was undertaken piece by piece, starting with housing and transportation, soon to be followed by an urban design plan and one for recreation and open space, then on to other important matters, such as seismic safety.

Have the long-range Master Plan elements themselves had enduring impacts on San Francisco's development? The answers are not always clear. Sometimes yes; sometimes no. The Embarcadero and Central freeways no longer exist, thanks in large measure to the 1989 Loma Prieta earthquake. But, by then, Master Plan policies had long since been established to demolish them, or certainly not to extend them, and a detailed plan done by the staff in 1974 was instrumental in showing how traffic could be made to work without the Embarcadero. Citywide plans called for giving preference to public transit over the automobile. Regarding housing, they called for a normative rather than concentrated distribution of moderate-income housing. It would be a stretch, though, to say that the Master Plan elements were the driving forces in activating those policies. Rather, a better claim can be made for the Urban Design Plan having had a significant impact on city development; but for only about 25 years, I fear.

Taking San Francisco's natural setting as a given – its street, block, and building scales, its development patterns, and its public spaces and buildings –

the Urban Design Plan is (I would rather not say "was") directed to the natures of future development. It is a plan to deal with the physical and sensory relationships between San Franciscans and their environment. So, one section addresses appropriate relationships of buildings to land and topography, the street system as a unifying and orienting element, landscaping, and open space, and the all-important views. "Conservation" is concerned with preserving unique natural areas, with maintaining the distinct characters of existing areas, and with preserving historic buildings. A powerful section on major new development includes guidelines for the location, height, bulk, shape, and orientation of new buildings. And a section on neighborhood improvement deals with a variety of measures to increase neighborhood livability, including ways to limit traffic in residential areas.

When first presented, in 1972 – with some fanfare in the form of an attractive document for people to take home with them – the plan was enormously popular and respected; so much so that people took to carrying it to meetings for many years, challenging those of us who had prepared it to make its proposals real. Legislation to implement the plan, in the form of citywide building height and bulk limits, historic districts to be honored and preserved, and new studies on sunlight and wind protection policies (by Peter Bosselmann at the University of California, Berkeley), soon followed on the heels of the plan's adoption.

To a considerable extent, private development in San Francisco followed the plan. The Hyatt Hotel at Union Square, a thin tower set behind modestly scaled buildings that respect the scale of the square, is a good example. The plan spurred other plans as well, such as the Recreation and Open Space Plan and a staff-advocated charter amendment that voters passed to tax themselves to carry it out. Other plans, like one for the downtown, followed; as did a fine, detailed design for Mission Bay (by John Kriken), sadly discarded.

The Urban Design Plan, and others of the Master Plan elements, has proven less effective in charting a course for public works initiatives than it did for influencing private development. The planners, after all, can have considerable control over the latter because they are much involved with regulations on land use through zoning. Collectively, however, they are but one of many players, and rarely possess a veto when it comes to public works. Their influence on the where and what of public development and project initiatives is more likely to come from their influence as ideas people who are respected by others as designers who might be talking sense. Having residents behind one's proposals certainly helps. But even the subject matter they so closely administer, presumably with the purpose of implementing the long-range city plan – that is, private uses of land and the physical forms of its development – can become very uncertain, depending on the political winds. Nonetheless, the late 1960s and early 1970s were notable for having established the idea of a Master Plan or general plan as a basis for regulation and for development decisions. People knew of the plan and what was in it, and a culture of having a plan and following it, or at least knowing when it was not being followed and why, was forcefully established. We will see, though, the fragility of such plans, even of the legislation that implements them, in the face of changing political winds.

We worked a lot with people, probably not to the satisfaction of citizen participation purists, theoreticians, or specialists in that art, but we were out there in the neighborhoods. For the most part, as when planning in the largely black and initially hostile South Bayshore area, we called well-advertised meetings, often by delivering notices to all individual mail-boxes, to get people together for an effort or to confront an issue. I didn't particularly like citizen advisory committees on the grounds that, once chosen, their members tended to become less representative and more elitist over time. We didn't agree to give any group or area a veto over anything we might propose, saying that if we proposed something they didn't like, they'd raise hell anyway at the City Planning Commission or at the Board of Supervisors. On occasion, when there were advisory committees, we would widely advertise all the meetings anyway. It took over a year of evening meetings, often confrontational, in the South Bayshore to gain acceptance in that neighborhood. A critical moment came one evening when I was challenged, even physically threatened, by a young man. With 30 or 40 residents sitting in the meeting, I thought it unwise to back down if we were to gain or retain credibility among them. The young man and I were soon shouting at each other. Adrenalin, being what it is, made his every pore and the whisker at its center sharply visible. He left in a huff, promising to get his friends at the local bar and show me whose community this really was. Scared to death, I tried to communicate through telepathy to the few staff sitting in the room to call the police, but that didn't work. Nothing bad happened, probably because the man couldn't find his friends at the bar. But at the next meeting and at many others that followed a very large fellow with forearms as big as my head – Sam Jordan – stood just inside the door. Though nothing was ever said, I concluded that Sam had been sent by the "community" to look after me. Later, I made friends with him. He ran his own bar and fine-catering service. A few months after the incident, neighborhood activists like Eloise Westbrook started calling to ask for advice on local matters and to invite me to mediate on neighborhood disagreements. I suspect that the earlier incident helped us.

For sure, not all, or even most, of the neighborhood meetings were contentious, and that was just as well. But many were. Those were contentious years. Truth is that the confrontations didn't bother me too much; they may even have suited my working style. I'm all for listening to people's concerns and to their needs and ideas for what ought to be done, and for some discussion leading. But at some point, fairly early in any city planning endeavor, ideas come to mind, opportunities, solutions, possible designs, call them hypotheses to be tested, if you will. As a so-called professional, I think I'm supposed to know something about my field, about what has worked and what hasn't, about what the data might mean, about ideas and alternative possibilities; and I'm supposed to do that with some dispatch, one of the qualities of a professional. And I have biases and make value judgments, presumably transparent, which are the reasons I have the job. And, yes, alternative ideas come early in the process. Generally, then, I have no problem with putting forth preliminary ideas, plans, and proposals as they surface. All of which can and did start disagreements at times, because maybe an early proposal seemed contrary to local concerns or unspoken notions of what ought to be, or because people wanted to air their grievances. But bandying about ideas, early on, often in some conflict among the participants, is a good way to smoke out, with speed, what really concerns people. The trick is not to become wedded to one's initial ideas.

Our outreach efforts led to many of the neighborhood meetings, but an equal number were requested by citizen groups with specific or general axes to grind. People like to see departmental heads, not just senior or junior staff, to talk candidly with the person in charge, even if that means venting one's spleen. Often they did just that. All of which was fine, unless things got nasty.

They did get nasty in the South of Market area one evening. Taking advantage of some federal funding that no other city department seemed to want, we quickly put together an application for a citywide urban mini-parks program, two of which could be in that area. Given federal deadlines, there wasn't time to have participation meetings with local residents before sending in the application. At an evening meeting called by a group of local residents who were well trained in harassment techniques, the shouting and accusations began as soon as we opened our mouths. One of these accusations held us personally responsible for the death of a young kid, hit by a car some months back. The discussion became loud and foul-mouthed, on my part as well as theirs. Strangely, amid all the screaming, perhaps because we were all really after the same thing – a couple of small, safe, open relaxation spaces in a neglected neighborhood – a new idea came, a shout for "QUIET," then a tense discussion and an agreement to meet in the department's offices on a particular date. The two mini-parks were duly built and they are still there. Might this positive conclusion have been achieved by more diplomatic, measured, less rancorous means? Possibly. But time was an issue and everyone being themselves worked, too, and with some dispatch.

A simple finding during those years: if you give people good, accurate, well-documented and clearly analyzed information, written so that reasonably intelligent people will easily understand it, in turn they will give you respect, and even some power. The information might be as simple as a map, with buildings and parcel lines shown. Information on yearly housing additions and tear-downs, prices, population changes and incomes were helpful to people and resulted, I'm sure, in their willingness to come to us to help plan their areas. I relearn that lesson today in professional practice. Having researched the physical, buildable characteristics that make the best streets, having published the findings in *Great Streets*, and having researched the qualities that make multi-way boulevards work with Elizabeth Macdonald and Yodan Rofe in *The Boulevard Book*, people think we're experts in street design. So they come to us to do just that. In time, the same was true for the Planning Department. It was also clear that people did not trust either the information or the analysis issued by the Redevelopment Agency or the traffic people, be they state or local. This helped us.

There are many ways to get a fix on the concerns of residents and business people regarding the development of their neighborhoods or the city as a whole in relation to such specific matters as freeways, as well as social issues. People at the weekly, public City Planning Commission meetings were very clear about what they liked and what they opposed in the way of proposed developments. It was easy to conclude that people hated the new "plastic apartments" that were replacing the older housing in the Richmond district, and that any proposed massive or quick physical change was likely to be met with resistance. More positively, in 1972, people's positive response to the Urban Design Plan pushed planning commissioners and supervisors alike to go further and faster than had been anticipated with laws to help implement the plan. Through the sense of community apparent at those weekly meetings, the information gathered through our outreach planning efforts in neighborhoods, and the understanding of issues gained by responding to neighborhood and interest groups' invitations to meetings, by the early 1970s, if asked by the Mayor or an individual supervisor, we could outline with some accuracy what the issues were, area by area. And some of them did indeed begin to ask, which reflected our growing stature in the community.

Always aware and proud that we worked for the people of the city, honored that the community had hired us to do its bidding, and never forgetting that the Planning Commission had hired and could fire me – figuratively, they signed my pay check – I saw our role as the professional staff as partners of people more than as facilitators. We were there to do more than merely listen and record. We were there to recommend what we thought was best.

Views down California Street from Nob Hill to the Bay Bridge are famous, as are views in the opposite direction. They remain because view corridors to the south of Market Street were established as a part of the city's Urban Design Plan. Appropriate city development is often not what is there to see but what is not there, and not to be experienced, in this case view-blocking development in those short corridors. The Embarcadero Freeway is no longer to be seen, nor is there a connection to it from the freeway (U.S. 280) that approached from the south, nor is there the double-decked Central Freeway that split the Octavia–Upper Market neighborhood and insulted the view of City Hall from the west. Old-time residents tend to forget functional and physical insults that once assailed their senses, such as the double-decked freeway in front of the Ferry Building. Newcomers don't know how fortunate they are not to be accosted by them. Those freeways were truly nasty structures: the first a dark, dank, noisy wall that kept people from the waterfront as well as development along it; the last, equally dark and foreboding, a physical and economic scar through a once

Central Freeway over Octavia Street

fine neighborhood under which ladies-of-the-evening and drug pushers could and did ply their trades. As was mentioned above, the Loma Prieta earthquake had a lot to do with their eradication, but so did good city planning and design.

Detailed design studies by the planning staff, completed in 1974, showed that the Embarcadero Freeway was of very doubtful necessity in the first place, that traffic could still work without it, that there were ways of handling vehicles while demolishing it, and that a connection to Route 280 from the south would be ill-advised. That the freeways were not retrofitted after the earthquake is due, to some considerable extent, to the analysis and designs of the staff. As for the Central Freeway, never-ending citizen activism was surely more important than professional advocacy of its removal, but the latter was also important. Appropriate development and new stores along Hayes Street are surely among the welcome consequences.

Along the Northern Waterfront, opposite Coit Tower, a most important and revered San Francisco icon, there is no high-rise hotel to dwarf the tower and make it effectively invisible. At a time when there were no height controls in that part of the city, we fought such a proposal with all our might and won. Nor, where the Levi-Strauss office campus sits along the waterfront, are there buildings to block the views of the shoreline, or views to Telegraph Hill. The Levi-Strauss people responded to what we asked of them. For a long time there was no high-rise, view-blocking development immediately north of the Bay Bridge, dwarfing the bridge and the views to and from it. Sadly, there are several now.

Regularly saying "no" to ill-conceived proposals, both public and private, if that is all or even much of what you do, or if that is the general perception of what you do, will soon create a lot of animosity and enemies, especially among elected officials, no matter how bad the proposals may be. Positive, imaginative proposals by staff are at least as important as undoing mistakes and nay-saying likely horrors; but, in the end, it may be only the city planner who remembers the bad stuff that was and is no longer there, and the inappropriate development that did not happen.

What do you do when your ability to make public projects and private developments actually happen is limited; when your "power" lies mostly in the regulatory realm and in policies and program ideas that others may choose not to carry out. You finagle and try to gain a bit of operational ability, and you try to influence others to do what you conclude is appropriate. With luck, and time, you get to affect a few tangible projects, some that even last and remain sources of satisfaction. They may be small in size, but that is of little matter. They are there to be seen, used, and hopefully enjoyed; that, after all, is what drove their doing. They can be reflected upon with joy.

We, the staff and myself, took advantage of funding possibilities from an urban beautification program, an initiative in the name of Lady Bird Johnson, the President's wife. No other department seemed to know of these funds, or how to use them; and when they did know, they weren't interested. So we got the funds and the ability to say how they would be used. As a result, Folsom Street is lined with Chinese elm trees, from Bernal Heights to near downtown, through the largely Latino Mission District. It is as long and continuous a double line of trees as there is to be found in San Francisco. Residents on parallel South Van Ness Street have said they'd like to have such lines of trees on their street. Most of the original plantings are still there. Yet we were warned, before work began, that the residents didn't value trees; that they were alien to their culture; that people would kill many of them. Nonsense!

We were able to respond to news that the historic South San Francisco Opera House, in South Bayshore, was in danger of being demolished by buying it. Neighborhood contacts like Ruel Brady and Eloise Westbrook agreed that saving it was a better and more urgent use of limited funds than the street trees we had programmed. The old Opera House remains as part of a community center, with an expanded public space alongside. It is not as well maintained as it might be, but it's there, good looking, and is part of the public realm, for people.

The mini-park on 24th Street, near York Street, remains as one of those small, often unnoticed public improvements that last and have meaning in the lives of local people. Of all the 24 mini-parks created, this one on 24th Street is particularly noteworthy. A difficult, hemmed-in site, it was enlivened by murals painted and later repainted by local artists on the walls of all the surrounding buildings. The murals reference Mexican and other Central American cultures and therefore those of local residents. Directed mostly to children's use in its 35-plus years of existence, it fell into disuse through lack of maintenance and partial takeover as a site for shady dealings. But, by 2006, it had re-emerged with new, appropriate, kid-inviting designs and sculpture by local artists.

Street improvements that accompanied subsidized home rehabilitation in the Duboce Triangle area, now associated with the Castro District, have lasted and stand as exemplars of how, with some ease, minor changes to streets and walks can help foster and maintain a sense of local community. The much-widened walks at corners, with places to sit and narrower streets, perpendicular rather than parallel curbside parking, street trees, a few planted in the centers of two streets, together provide a physical setting that invites people to get together and make more improvements of their own invention. They have become exemplars for people in other neighborhoods to say what they want for theirs, and they do: "We want what was done in the Duboce Triangle area."

A neighborhood planning effort in Chinatown resulted in a small housing development for moderate-income people, together with community services. We proposed it as a very limited redevelopment project (with no displacement of residents), one that the Redevelopment Agency did not fully support (too small for them and requiring some local money). By the mid-1970s, though, elected officials were listening to the Planning Department at least as much as to the Redevelopment Agency, so the rather successful and nicely designed project stands.

To one very much concerned with the physical environment of urban places, particularly in relation to the quality of people's lives, small improvements

Street and pedestrian area improvements, Duboce Triangle Area, San Francisco

that remain, that can be seen and touched, improvements that one might have had something to do with, are more than a little satisfying. That they are visible examples of good city planning is more to the point.

San Francisco's setting, its topography, its vistas and celebrated bridges notwithstanding, you don't want to look too closely at its streets. For far too many of them, "bleak" and "barren" are appropriate descriptors; for commercial and residential streets alike, very much the latter. Qualities that lead to this condition are wide rights-of-way and auto emphasis, wide and unrelieved sidewalks, an extraordinary number of curb-cut driveways to enter blank garage doors, leaving precious little space for landscaping, telephone poles and overhead wires, and a general lack of trees, the wrong trees, or a haphazard approach to tree planting that negates a positive impact. Building façades, particularly the Victorians, the generally unified design of the Marina District, and the set-back houses of Forest Hills and St. Francis Woods, and parts of Pacific Heights, can add interest and make up for the bareness, but these are exceptions. Individual streets, like Dolores Street, are also quite worthy, but they hardly overcome the relentless grids of the Outer Sunset, much of Richmond, the outer Mission areas, and the Bayview, areas where not-so-wealthy people live.

The sad nature of the streets was readily apparent, at least to me. Truth be told, changing them for the better, except in areas like the Duboce Triangle and a few others where we were doing neighborhood plans, was not a high citywide priority. Why not? Answers are easy, but may not be sufficient. We had to be active in rebuffing Department of Public Works attempts to widen streets and to create more one-way streets. People in the Sunset area actively opposed the idea of street trees – they felt, maybe correctly, that there was little enough sun as it was – and some argued that trees created sidewalk mess, which was a new one to me. Then there was the matter of what could be done on a broad scale to overcome all those curb cuts, the utilities running under the sidewalks, and the costs. Who would pay and why favor one area over another? An answer may be that people don't see problems if they don't also see solutions and opportunities for betterment. But that should be a role of the planner: to see early on what others might not and to inspire satisfying alternatives to what is not so good.

Our citywide proposals for neighborhood improvements in the Urban Design Plan and traffic-calming proposals notwithstanding, we could have done better. There are many ways to change barren streets into truly desirable public places, perhaps most of which, for San Francisco, involve less concrete and asphalt and more plants (not only trees). Since the 2000s, the Better Streets Plan of the current City Planning Department, in cooperation with other departments, has gone much further than we did and some early results are promising. It helps that people are more environmentally aware now than they were in the 1960s and 1970s.

It would be pushing reality to suggest that the citywide visions for growth and development included in the Master Plan elements that we completed have had the long-term staying power that was intended. Wonderfully received when

Duboce Triangle area, San Francisco

first presented, and highly influential in the years immediately following its completion, the Urban Design Plan was much less important as a guide to or determinant of city development in the first decade of the new millennium.

The turning point seems to coincide with changes to the city charter and with the election of Willie Brown as Mayor in the mid-1990s. The charter changes gave more powers to the Mayor, perhaps as part of a national movement to encourage stronger, presumed to be more efficient and responsible, chief executives. Brown, a long-term veteran of partisan politics at the state level, very connected to the development community and to San Francisco's liberal power-brokers, wealthy and minority alike, knew how to take advantage of these changes. Appointed planning commissioners knew they were beholden to the Mayor, as was the new director of city planning, a person not overly trained in the field. They had their marching orders: get the projects approved, and none of that environmental or urban design or long-range nonsense. So-called professionals and appointed citizen commissioners paid attention.

By the late 1990s, there were many new people in and coming to San Francisco, many of them young, and many associated with the new Silicon Valley-inspired technologies, few of whom were conversant with or sympathetic to the city's development history or its physical environmental values: the new pragmatists. Older city activists seemed less vigorous, or were just plain tired; and there was a new group of land-use lawyers and those who made a living as "expeditors" to serve the needs of a high-rolling, speculative development community, many of whom had close links with his honor. Peter Svirsky had long since retired. Moreover, much of the proposed new development would come in areas not normally associated with the city's most cherished physical history, but in downtown or new areas where activists would be less knowing, less caring, and more prone to say, "Let them have it. If we say nothing, we won't be seen as against everything and can be more powerful where it counts most – in *our* neighborhood." So people came out in big numbers to protest (successfully) against a law-changing building proposal near Telegraph Hill and North Beach. But they were largely silent with respect to the equally bad, or worse, affair next to the Bay Bridge.

One way to get around legislation passed to implement a plan – building height and bulk legislation, for example – is to engage in publicly sponsored redevelopment projects that create new, higher, or greater-size possibilities under the guise of being well-thought-out, detailed designs controlled by the public after all, wiping out the older limits. My experience has been that when push comes to shove, city redevelopment agencies in the U.S. really don't care much about citywide urban planning or city design, and see planning departments as impediments to their projects – similar viewpoints to those held by large private property developers. Another way to circumvent plans is simply to change the zoning, not necessarily a tough trick with a staff leader who takes his or her marching orders from the Mayor's staff.

So what?

In the vicinity of the Bay Bridge, the Urban Design Plan calls for buildings to be no higher than the height of the lower deck of the bridge, the idea being that in a community where views of and from the city are of prime importance, they should not be blocked upon entering or leaving. And that was the law. Furthermore, the bridge itself is an icon, not with the drama and stand-out color of the Golden Gate Bridge, but certainly every bit as important in defining San Francisco, and with its own disappearing act into Yerba Buena Island. Far more people use it rather than the Golden Gate. It has stood alone, magnificent in its own right, a landmark to be seen and admired. No more! The new high-rise residential towers on either side of the bridge approaches – one truly high, at 80-plus floors – now block many of those views. More buildings are promised. The visual space between the bay, the bridge, and downtown will disappear. A long-time local power-broker, supposedly a city planner, expounds in defense of those particular towers that they and others to come are fine. They remind him of Chicago, from where he hails. Of course, this fails to understand that San Francisco is not Chicago, and nor should it be.

City planning, in general, and urban design in particular, have to do with context: at the metropolitan region, citywide, or large area scales, they are almost by definition concerned with wholeness and with relationships, partic-ularly with the natural and man-made environments, as well as with societal values. Why do a plan otherwise? Why think ahead, which is what a plan purportedly does? As long as an "I don't do context" mentality is the mantra of the smart folks of the early 21st century – particularly the celebrity architects (and those who would be) and the big-time developers – then citywide urban design plans will be in trouble.

The largest new development area in San Francisco is the so-called Mission Bay area, south of the downtown. Despite an earlier, well-conceived plan for the area, by John Kriken – one that honored the height limits and the scale of San Francisco – what has been built are bulky, view-stopping buildings and, further south, large, single-structure blocks with few building entrances and little of interest for pedestrians at street level.

If there is a lesson in all of this – and I have given but a few of many possible examples of inappropriate development that should never have happened – it is that greed, when allowed to flourish, trumps good city design every time.

But greed does not explain the newest federal office building. In 1967, soon after arriving in San Francisco, I commented to Herb Caen, the city's long-time tastemaker-columnist, that the then-newish federal building must surely be the worst building in the city, with its bleak, slab-like bulk that created such wind currents at its base as to make it hard for people to stand, and necessary to shut off the fountains on the unused plaza. Herb printed what I said and got me in trouble with John Carl Warnecke, the building's designer, who did what most architects would do when faced with such criticism: blamed it on the client. But Warnecke's federal building, rendered "less bad" by Skidmore, Owings and Merrill's façade for the state office building in front of it, is nothing when compared to Thom Mayne's new federal building. If ever there was a building that didn't care to fit in with its surroundings, or care if it blocked views, or care if it imposed itself with enormous bulk and a lack of any rhythm or grace upon the city, then this is it. It is like the feds are saying, "If you didn't like what we did to you last time, try this!" Sure, neither the feds nor the state authorities are compelled to abide by city standards, but an active, forceful, "We are here and you'd better damned well listen to us and pay attention to what we want" professional staff could have made a difference. After all, the state was prevailed upon to follow city planning–design mandates as regards to the University of California's medical school expansion proposals in the 1970s, as were the feds in regard to new buildings in the Presidio. Maybe such matters are simply no longer of any importance to the city's planners.

Elements of San Francisco's Master Plan from the late 1960s and early 1970s – for housing, transportation, urban design, and recreation and open space – were well prepared, well written, and presented in language that was easily understandable. They responded to real issues, perceived as such by a commending public. The Urban Design Plan, perhaps most of all, was in tune with widely held values and concerns, as demonstrated repeatedly in public meetings and in the insistence that it should be carried out. To this observer, it is clearly less important as a driving force in guiding the city's development in 2010 than it was until the mid-1990s. There seem to be many reasons, some already mentioned, which may account for a certain shakiness and crap-shoot nature of much long-range planning for cities whose initial physical structure has been long established, with the non-planning perspective of most mayors high among them. For Mayor Brown, anything that got in the way of an ability to wheel and deal with development and developers seems to have been shunned. I think this is only to be expected of a big city mayor. If power within local government is focused on a strong chief executive, then forceful long-range physical development policy becomes something of a hit-or-miss prospect. That is what seems to have happened in San Francisco. It is particularly unfortunate, in my estimation, that the various mayors have failed to realize that the city has been in what the economists might call a "sellers' market" for granting development for a long time. That is, people – particularly land developers, would-be residents, and firms – have wanted to locate in the city. Within reason, it made sense to require strong building rules that would be adhered to, and would not be open to easy manipulation.

Notwithstanding the nature of cities' mayors, sustained, active, even militant citizen activism can be a very powerful ally for the values reflected and foreseen in master plans. A perceived likelihood of being thrown out of office can be a strong influence on mayors and council members alike. But populations change. The older warhorses have less energy and those newly in the race need to be brought along, learn to understand the course, which is not always an easy trick. Then, too, it is much easier to support and defend a plan and its principles if major new developments are reasonably close at hand, even visible, or in areas well known and cherished. Much of the recent worst development in San Francisco is either at the fringes of downtown, but south of Market Street, or further south, associated with the new ball park or Mission Bay. "Out of sight, out of mind" applies. Bring to North Beach or to the foot of Telegraph Hill some of the giants already near the Bay Bridge or under construction or planned in that vicinity, and one can almost guarantee citizen-led hell breaking out.

The professional staff is not without fault in regard to bringing about a strong reaction to long, involved, and costly case-by-case reviews of individual development proposals. Property owners have a right to know what they can and cannot do on their properties through basic legislation having to do with land uses, height, bulk, perhaps parking, and frontage on public streets: qualities that can be specified without equivocation and written into legislation, and easily verified at a public counter by a trained person. Sure, bad, even offensive, buildings and land development will still happen, but that is and always will be possible. The ability to design poorly is manifest under any and all regulations and guidelines. Every building proposal should not be a special case. But, to a considerable extent, that seems to be what happened in the late 1970s and beyond, and a strong developer- and lawyer-driven anti-city-planning reaction in favor of "big" and "now" was predictable.

It makes sense to reconsider city plans, perhaps not according to some predetermined schedule, but at least on an as-needed time clock. The Urban Design Plan was followed as a major guide and determinant of physical development for over 20 years after its presentation. Most of the implementing legislation is still in place and the plan's principles are followed in day-to-day developments. It is the big screw-ups – the Mayne-designed federal office buildings and the big "thing" at the entrance to the Bay Bridge – that raise my hackles most and remind me of what is being lost and what might have been. Who will remember the satisfying environments that have been lost? Perhaps it is time for a reconsideration of that plan, or at least a reminder to San Franciscans of the plans that do exist and why they remain important. Perhaps San Francisco's current residents would not support the Urban Design Plan. A reconsideration would soon find out, particularly one that would address what should remain of the existing plan and what might be changed, to reflect new realities: a long-range approach revisited rather than ad hoc redevelopment.

People, as individuals or in groups, can make a difference in getting things done (or stopping them) at the local level. Or, even if they do not get things done, they are remembered because they make urban life and working in the city rich and full. Eloise Westbrook, early and forceful leader in the South Bayshore area, was such a person. One also comes across less-than-admirable people in the job I had – truly greedy people who have no trouble lying and don't bat an eyelid when confronted with their perfidy, or the well-to-do and well-placed movers and shakers who say all the right things but are no help when needed. But I'd rather remember the good guys whose memory can bring a smile – the likes of Sam

Jordan, and the kids of his neighborhood who would yell out to me, "Hey, Mister Clean, watcha' doin' here today?"

Having worked hard for over two years to develop a plan for the South Bayshore area – meeting after meeting, overcoming local hostility, training staff, getting to know people well – we were ready. We first presented the plan in the South San Francisco Opera House, which would be saved from demolition; then, more formally, to the Planning Commission for consideration and adoption as part of the city's Master Plan. Trouble was that only people from the adjoining "Little Hollywood" area showed up for the first presentation, and they didn't like many of our recommendations, particularly those dealing with moderate-income housing and a new shoreline park. I was concerned. What had all those evening meetings gained us? Then, at the second, crucial presentation, people of the neighborhood showed up in large numbers to tell the commissioners to adopt the plan; it was theirs, the neighborhood's, not ours. On the way out of that successful meeting, Eloise Westbrook stopped me and said with a big smile, "Had you worried, didn't we, Jacobs."

Mortimer Fleishhacker – wealthy, very reserved, conservative, Republican – was everything that an appointed public person should be. He read everything we sent to the commissioners, held meetings to discuss our coming proposals, asked tough, pertinent questions, and quietly spent money to help important causes. He served on committees and came to the evening neighborhood meetings in Chinatown, often with Janet, his wife. When we were having trouble with the army and the Presidio general who wanted to do things contrary to our guidelines for development, it was Mort (I called him Mr. Fleishhacker to his face) who called the Secretary of Defense to set him and the general straight. In the process of setting new height limits for downtown (the first ever), a very wealthy property owner complained loudly of restrictions and confiscation without compensation, as he saw it. Mort, in the public meeting, asked the man if he had seen him that morning at the stock exchange.

"Yes."

"Do you buy and sell stocks?"

"Yes."

"After you buy stocks, does their value sometimes go up and sometimes go down?"

"Yes."

"Mine, too. What makes you think it's any different with real property?"

Silence and a withering look which suggested that the man thought Mort was a traitor to his class.

Alvin Duskin, then a local dress manufacturer, got enough signatures to put a referendum on the ballot that would have limited all buildings in the city to 72 feet. The Chamber of Commerce spent a lot of money to defeat that proposal. Soon after, Peter Haas, head of the Levi Strauss Company, called to ask if he could come to see me. Had I still been living in Cleveland or Pittsburgh, the question would have been whether *I* could come to see *him*. In my office on the appointed date, Haas revealed that he had just spent a lot of his firm's money supporting the anti-Duskin campaign; that he didn't like spending money that way; and that the people who bought his firm's jeans might not like it too much either. He was familiar with our design plan and said that it made sense to him. Then he asked how he could help us. To me, that was an amazing offer. In what other large city would something like that happen? In what other city would the head of a major corporation have knowledge of a design plan? I said that he undoubtedly moved in different circles to mine, so initially it would help if he could talk up our plan and any follow-up legislation among his acquaintances. Then, perhaps he could host a luncheon for the big business people in town; I would also attend, to further the plan. The lunch never proved necessary.

Dorothy Erskine – a classic Bay Area little old lady, with white hair, tennis shoes, and a green thumb – would call early in the morning, before I left for the office. "Allan, why did you recommend this and what about that? Don't you think such-and-such is a problem? Shouldn't we do something else? When can we start? I'll call so-and-so today and have him call you." Dorothy was an advocate for low- and moderate-income housing and a fierce conservationist. Meetings of People for Open Space were hosted at her home early on. She had done or sponsored studies to determine the smallest economic vineyard in the Napa Valley and then pushed legislation to make that size the minimum for a one-family home. The existence of Napa Valley vineyards owes much to Dorothy. She was always on at me. After one of our meetings, she made her house available to a work group that prepared a city charter addition that would establish a modest, 15-year tax to implement our recently completed Recreation and Open Space Plan. She gave money to help further the cause. The measure passed. I would have been happy to have more people like Dorothy constantly on at me. Late in her life, one day in a swimming pool near Calistoga, talking together, she told me that two of the good things about getting older were that one has suffered so many defeats that the prospect of another doesn't bother you, and that you feel free to say what you believe and advocate likewise.

Residents of the Alamo Square area were fearful of and skeptical about a subsidized code enforcement program we were proposing for their area. Rents might rise as a result, and lower-income folks might well be displaced. We did a detailed study of incomes, rents, and changes in the latter in similar areas and found that the fears were justified for people in two blocks. However, we envisaged no problems in the many other blocks. We advised the residents of our findings, including how we did the study, and suggested removal of the two affected blocks from the project area. The surprising response was, essentially, "No, keep the blocks in. With your program, some of us might get hurt, but we know what we're getting. Leave us out and the redevelopment program might well get us all." It proved to be a successful effort and, to my knowledge, no one was forced to move because of rent increases.

Willie Brown was not the best thing that ever happened to San Francisco's city planning program – far from it – but he did help preserve a major open space as a park at the city's southeastern entrance. Earlier, when he was a very big presence in California's legislature, during Ronald Reagan's governorship, he sent an aide to some hearings on our Recreation and Open Space Plan, to testify in favor of it. To me, it was a grandstanding gesture, and I told him so at a meeting arranged in his office. Why not use his position to get the city a new state park along the bay waterfront, in the South Bayshore area, where poor folks lived? He agreed and, after hearings in Sacramento and possibly through his links with Reagan's people, monies were allocated for the park. It is not well maintained, is largely unknown, and is uncelebrated (particularly when compared with any part of the Golden Gate National Recreation Area along the Pacific coast, where middle- and higher-income people live). But it is still there, and much more can become of it.

Jim Kearney, a long-time planning commissioner, was a longshoreman, unloading ships, and was often president of the local, very powerful union. President or not, he never stopped working the ships, yet he was always present at the commission meetings. When Alcatraz, the infamous prison island in the bay, was finally deactivated and became surplus federal property, available for development, there was a rush of proposals, not the least of which was for a space museum with a tower and maybe even a statue of Werner Von Braun. Picture that: Werner Von Braun to be gazed at from Telegraph Hill and gazing back. Elected officials became entrepreneurs overnight, it seemed, or proponents of friends' ideas. The feds had big ideas, too, with visions of the big money people would offer for the rights to develop. I had to remind them that the city had the power to zone the land for whatever it wished, including single-family housing, and they backed off a bit. In a very touching moment at a commission meeting, Kearney made the only proposal that, to me, made any sense. The island, he said, represented the worst of man. It was a terrible, hope-draining place in a spectacular setting, a prison that should never have been built; perhaps as much a statement about the nastiness of the jailors, and society, as of the jailed. He proposed doing nothing with it: let the island rot and crumble over time, become ruins, to serve as a reminder of the dark side of both perpetrators of crime and their keepers. It would have been better to listen to Jim Kearney than to turn Alcatraz into a tourist destination.

For sure, positive citizen activism remains alive in the city. Robin Leavitt and the late Patricia Walkup, along with a host of Hayes Valley residents, worked tirelessly to bring about the destruction of the hated Central Freeway and for its replacement with Octavia Boulevard. Even as I write there are calls from Robin to let me know the most recent administrative/regulatory attacks on the boulevard by the Department of Parking and Traffic and to enlist support to combat them.

In an earlier book, *Making City Planning Work*, I suggested that cities are the first line of government for most people. They feel their problems and frustrations where they live and work, and it is in their communities where they state their expectations and lodge their complaints. It is possible to do city planning within a context of specific faces and names as well as of places and things, to relate abstract ideas and plans to tangible experiences. The people, so many of them, and especially the fine ones, endure.

I can only wonder about the impact of Proposition 13 on San Francisco's development since the mid-1970s, when it was passed in California, and on the city's plans and ideas for its future. That voter-enacted referendum, it will be remembered, basically froze local property taxes. A personal consequence, as an example, is that I pay about the same taxes in the city as I recently paid for a condominium one-third the size in Vancouver.

Ironically, during my last year as San Francisco's planning director, just before Proposition 13, we put together a proposal, for local voters' approval, to tax themselves a small amount for 15 years in order to provide the funding for our recently completed Recreation and Open Space Plan, with priority to be given to designated high-need areas. It passed. People were prepared to tax themselves so that proposals which they believed would improve the city could be implemented.

Money is harder to come by now, even to maintain basic services, let alone to implement city improvement plans. Now, large-scale developments, to be assessed and taxed at their current values rather than pre-Proposition 13 rates, promise more income, and for that reason alone they may be more acceptable than might have been the case. This at the same time as the city is less willing or able to press ahead with major improvements on its own behalf and in parts of the city that are less celebrated than where the money is. Perhaps it was easier to be an activist planning director in the 1960s and 1970s than it is today. However, I can't help but think that people would still be willing to pay for the implementation of well-thought-out, exciting plans and programs that have been clearly and honestly presented to them.

If developers in San Francisco, particularly those of major private projects, have managed to thumb their noses in recent years at approved long-range plans, and if much less than one might have wished or intended is now reality, which physical changes might be celebrated? Particularly, which appropriate developments have followed from all the planning? The demise of the freeways has been noted, as has some of the good that followed in their place. And, along with Elizabeth Macdonald and others, it is nice to have had more than a little to do with the design of Octavia Boulevard and the park, Patricia's Green, that terminates it. But those came later, in a different professional life. It does strike me, though, that small, visible, buildable, touchable, mostly public projects last and set models for future works, illustrate what could be, and mean a lot to the people for whom they were designed, and to others. The long line of trees along Folsom Street does that, as do the trees and public spaces of the Duboce Triangle area, which residents have taken over and improved beyond what was foreseen. The small, moderate-income housing and community center re-development project just past the Stockton Tunnel in Chinatown that grew out of our planning efforts is another. The South San Francisco Opera House and the State Park at Candlestick Point followed directly from citywide and neighborhood planning efforts. Little things can mean a lot.

I conclude, looking back, that having operational ability to control some funds, even very small amounts, to direct how they may be spent, presumably to implement plans as well as to take advantage of unexpected opportunities, is extremely important as a mechanism to make plans and policies become reality. Where we were successful entrepreneurs in terms of getting our hands on funds whose use we might at least partially control – for mini-parks, for code enforcement combined with minor public improvements, for urban beautifi-cation, for state funds to build a specific project, for the city charter amendment to pay for recreation and park improvements – there are "things" that still exist and which have had positive, hopefully long-lasting local meaning. But what if we had been able to gain control of more funds? Would we have become more entrepreneurial and less planning oriented; more like my view of the Redevelopment Agency? Maybe. Who knows?

The most positive, dramatic change to San Francisco over the last 30-plus years is the northern and northeastern waterfront, from the Golden Gate Bridge to the kids' mini-baseball diamond–park at McCovey Cove, a distance of about seven miles. Crissy Field, a gem of a restoration area, part of the Golden Gate National Recreation Area, has rightfully become a huge draw for walkers, cyclists, skaters, picnickers, fishermen, beachgoers, naturalists, people of all ages, and dogs. Then, moving east, comes the long-established Marina Green and Fort Mason and the not-for-profit institutions that occupy old navy warehouses and barracks that were once points of departure for young people and goods heading for the Pacific in World War II. The walk along the bluff of the park reminds walkers and cyclists alike that this is a hilly city, even at the water's edge. The public fishing pier that ends Van Ness Avenue, the historic Maritime Museum at Hyde Street, and the touristy Fisherman's Wharf area come next; tourists, yes, but with choices of some fine fish eateries. This area presents a wonderful obstacle course for a cyclist determined to get from one end of the seven-mile stretch to the other. Then, past old piers and along a relatively newly developed Embarcadero roadway to the restored Ferry Building, at the foot of Market Street, a major destination now that the freeway is gone. Far from finished, this pathway along the water's edge moves south from the Ferry Building, on to the new ball park, a fine promenade with views of the bay, the Bay Bridge, and on to Berkeley, Oakland, and the hills beyond. The name of the ball park seems to change yearly, but it is a stroke of genius in terms of location – along the water, eminently reachable by public transit, a livening destination even in winter when there are no games. Across the Third Street drawbridge over China Basin and along the McCovey Cove lineal park, the promenade ends at a sitting area next to what might be the best miniature baseball diamond ever dreamed up.

Pieces of this long waterfront attraction were planned well in advance, for sure, most notably the Embarcadero roadway from Fisherman's Wharf to

Octavia Boulevard, San Francisco

the ball park, but not as a unit and not as a result of a conscious plan, certainly not by the Planning Department. Our job was to work to stop freeway connections and to get the Embarcadero Freeway removed and replaced by a surface route. In this, our planning was on target and more than helpful. The wonderful irony of the wholeness of the public waterfront is that much of it is the result of many separate, largely uncoordinated, mostly public projects, while giving due credit to the Port Authority's plans. Unlike Vancouver's magnificent public waterfront promenade that travels from North False Creek, past the West End, around Stanley Park, and then along Coal Harbour's edge, and now along South False Creek as well, which has been planned and consciously designed, and which follows long-established city policy, San Francisco's new, hard-edged, waterfront wholeness has evolved largely by luck. At least, though, we gave luck a chance.

In a city such as San Francisco – where the street pattern and block sizes are long established, and where most of the physical changes are likely to be incremental – it would be easy and perhaps reasonable to conclude that large, major-change initiatives are not in order, that fitting in is more appropriate, and that matters of sunlight, wind, environmental responsibility, and local historic importance (very much including views and view corridors) should be the foci of strong public policies. And yet . . . Think of Golden Gate Park and its long southern edge that makes no gesture to the city that adjoins it, not even a welcoming parkside promenade. Or think of Park Presidio and Sunset Boulevard, each flanked by unused, unwelcoming, block-wide wildernesses along both sides. Imagine them as active, lineal park strips, every bit as attracting and active as Ocean and Eastern parkways in Brooklyn; even, over time, lined with dense but modestly scaled housing for a wide variety of people. The mind, at least my mind, boggles at the possibilities. If the life of strong, long-range, citywide plans is tenuous at best, given the crap-shoot nature of those who are likely to hold public office, and given the development pressures combined with slick greed in a city like San Francisco, there are at least many opportunities for well-designed public projects to be conceived and made real, making life better for newcomers and old timers alike. We managed, I think, to get a few of them done.

The Civil Service Giants

Having left as San Francisco's planning director in favor of a teaching and research role at the University of California, Berkeley, I had a chance, finally, to say what I thought to be the insanities of what was then the city's civil service system; an exposé. Instead of a long, academic research undertaking, I ended up writing my first short story about that system. Lucky me, *Harpers* magazine published it. It follows, only slightly changed from the original.

The San Francisco Giants went civil service in 1980. The team – the players, the managers, the coaches, the batboys, and the grounds keepers – all of them became civil service employees of the City and County of San Francisco that year. It wasn't planned.

After an unexpectedly good year in 1978, when the Giants actually finished third after leading for most of the season, the team fell to fifth place in 1979. Attendance, which had exploded in 19'78, sank to 1,500–3,000 on weekdays and 10,000–12,000 on weekends when the Dodgers were in town. So the local owner sold the Giants near the end of the 1979 season to a Brazilian who had made it big selling Amazonian hardwoods in Georgia and was looking for his own tax shelter. The new owner soon found out about major-league salaries, all those empty seats, and the other competition that was bidding for the fans' dollars in the Bay Area. He concluded that maybe he hadn't bought the best baseball franchise in the world, tax write-off or not, and began thinking and talking of moving the team, just as earlier owners had when fans stayed away from games. He felt sure he could break the Giants' lease arrangement for the use of Candlestick Park.

By now, few people paid much attention to that sort of posturing and threats to leave. Those antics made good press for a day or two, but it was well known that the Giants were locked into San Francisco for 20 years by virtue of an ironclad agreement they had signed with the city's Department of Parks and Recreation. Some long-forgotten lawyer in the city attorney's office had written a lease that bound the two parties together like Siamese twins. The city attorney always got a bit antsy when the Giants threatened to leave. He asked a new, young assistant, Hadrian Ness, fresh from the University of San Francisco Law School, to check up on it: could the Giants get out of the lease? The assignment had been given before and was considered good training by the old pros in the office. Ness was eager to make his mark and took the job more seriously than his predecessors had. He also had no other assignments just then and wanted to be busy, lest some city councilman demand that his position be lopped off the payroll. City attorneys were about the only category of employees in San Francisco that didn't have civil service protection, and that rankled Ness. After all, the rest of his University of San Francisco Law School classmates who went to work for the city (some 68 percent was said to be the yearly average) were secure for life. Ness was pretty angry about that.

In his research, Ness made some interesting observations. He noticed that the lease was with the Department of Parks and Recreation, not with the city council or the Mayor or the city. He recalled that the city charter said something about all Park–Rec employees having to be hired through the civil service. Ness also observed that the Giants' front office worked in space in Candlestick Park provided by Park–Rec. Some of the Giants' personnel were pretty chummy with the Park–Rec people. After all, they shared the same johns. On a few occasions (once when there had been a printers' strike in town, and once when someone had forgotten to reorder envelopes) the Giants had sent out letters on Park–Rec stationery. What are friends for? Apparently, Willy Mays' contract had once been sent with a letter that bore Park–Rec's seal. The head of Park–Rec had framed a photocopied facsimile, and hung it on the wall behind his desk.

From these seemingly innocent observations and from one day seeing the Giants' groundskeepers digging up the pitcher's mound, raking the base paths, and cutting the infield grass – the kind of thing that the city's own gardeners did – Ness came to a startling conclusion: all of the team, including the players, were employees of the City and County of San Francisco, and should be treated as such! Assuming Ness was right, that meant that, like all Park–Rec staff, the players would have to be hired by civil service procedures. Among other things, they would have to pass exams, and any new players would have to live in the city. Fantastic! Ness's father, a union organizer/street cleaner working for the city at $50,000 a year, not bad in 1980, would be proud of him.

Ness went immediately to his boss to tell him the exciting news, but that august personage was out defending the city on a zoning case. So, while waiting, Ness had lunch with his newfound city hall friend, reporter Russ Clone. He confided to Clone the significance of what he had found, knowing without having to ask that his friend would treat the matter confidentially.

The story that hit the afternoon papers was headlined CITY ATTORNEY SAYS GIANTS CIVIL SERVICE. The Mayor was quoted on the evening news as asking, "Did the city attorney say that?" San Francisco, as any political science student will tell you, had a weak-mayor form of government. Then Governor Brown the Younger, reached at a San Francisco ashram, thought it was a good idea, but if this was just another ploy of San Francisco politicians to get state money in the post-Proposition 13 era, they had another guess coming. He said he hadn't been born yesterday, you know. The commissioner of baseball said something to the effect that this was probably just another bit of nonsense coming out of San Francisco and needn't be taken seriously. He thought that San Francisco ought to start trying to solve its baseball problems instead of coming up with such insanities.

Hadrian Ness didn't think it was funny. He took his severance pay and, with a small grant from the Civil Service Foundation, set up an office and brought the matter to court. Ness also managed to get an injunction against the Giants – or anyone else for that matter – using Candlestick Park until the case was settled. So a lot of people wanted the question resolved quickly. Anticipating appeals, the city and the Giants agreed to let the matter go directly to the California Supreme Court, where it was heard in late January of 1980.

The young grandson of one of the justices had just been traded by the Giants to a Cincinnati farm team in Tennessee. The justice didn't know where Tennessee was, was sure the boy had never been given a chance, felt the whole business of buying and trading players was akin to slavery, and feared he'd never see his favorite grandson again. By a one-vote margin, the California Supreme Court agreed with Ness: the Giants had to be civil service.

San Francisco's ball team became the laughing stock of baseball in a flash, well before the first pitch of the 1980 season. Baseball, like most other professional sports, was big business. Most fans knew that *where* the team played had almost nothing to do with the team itself. Place was incidental to the business/sport, a vestige of an older, more romantic time when the owners also owned breweries and the players might even live on the next street. In the modern era, the players had almost never grown up in the cities where they played. They came from places like Cuba and Mexico. Only the bat boys lived in the home city.

It was an era of trades, options, release clauses, free agency, multi-year contracts, and making it while you could. Game times and places were deter-mined more by the imagined needs of a preprogrammed national television audience than by local preference. Most people suspected that national and international TV ran sports anyway. It was clear that a local team, made up of local civil servants who came from and lived in San Francisco, could never compete in an international sport.

The players were dumbfounded. Civil service? Civil servants? They had only recently been given some freedom from the odious "reserve clause" that bound them for life to whichever team owned their contracts. They were making lots of money now that they were almost free to play for the highest bidder. Players knew that civil servants didn't make much money; no one called a civil servant could. So they quickly turned to their lawyers, agents, and contracts. There was understandable confusion amid the facts and rumors that did the rounds. Old contracts would have to be honored, wouldn't they? Players could play out their options and then try to land with another team – but who would want them? Would there be pay cuts? The lawyers and the agents had a windfall of unexpected fees and commissions while looking after their players' interests. They felt secure in advising the latter to take it easy and see how things sorted themselves out. The season was about to start, and in all likelihood they would be secure for the year.

Player security was actually enhanced when Giants' manager Grubb tried to fire his third-base coach just before the season started. The coach had a drinking problem and was wobbly on the field three out of five days. He kept sending base runners home from second base on ground balls hit to the infield – the runners were always out by 40 feet. And Grubb had found out that the coach was having an affair with his wife. So Grubb fired the bounder, who promptly appealed to the Civil Service Commission.

Bernice D'Orsi, head of the civil service, advised her commissioners that drunkenness on the job, during games, had not been proved (Grubb wondered how you could prove that), that the coach sent the runners home on his best professional judgment and it was his judgment against the manager's (who, by sitting in the dugout, was farther from the actual scene of action), and that the wife-stealing business was personal, not professional and work-related. Grubb should certainly be able to make that simple distinction and not carry over a private relationship into the work environment. D'Orsi therefore recommended against the firing and was upheld unanimously by the Commission. Grubb was dazed by the experience. He had always been able to fire coaches at will. It was one of his few pleasures. Worse yet, now that the business about his wife and the coach was out in the open, he would have to move out of his apartment. He had never had to do that before. He locked himself in the manager's office for three days and then looked for a new place to live.

Hearing the news, some old-time players who were barely hanging on, as well as some rookies not quite out of the minor leagues but praying never to go back to the Fresnos of the world, were seen walking into the office of the civil service union.

As strange as it may seem, the totally bizarre circumstances of the Giants began to have a positive effect on the team's fortunes. The first sign was when it became apparent that there was a hard knot of fans that showed up at most home games and sat together, isolated out in the right-field stands. These 1,000 or so people were readily defined by all the vacant seats around them. They were, of course, civil servants. They took advantage of cheap tickets available to them as part of a promotion to stave off financial disaster and came every night. They soon found out that the afternoon rest-break that the union had won for them could be stretched into four or five innings on day games. They were a happy, fun-loving bunch who soon got to know and like each other, and found Candlestick Park a good place to hold informal meetings to discuss working conditions and wages. They cheered on their union brothers in uniform, regardless of how the game was going or of how badly their heroes played. They were a positive crowd.

San Francisco's civil service fans helped, but not enough to make any difference. It was the nature of San Franciscans that made a difference. Remember, San Franciscans are the kind of people who voted for McGovern, legalizing pot, legalizing abortion, and the rights of homosexuals, and against Jarvis–Gann tax legislation, the death penalty, and a lot of other things that later became important. To some of them, in July, the notion of their local team competing against the national and international impersonal institution that baseball had become gave the whole matter a David-and-Goliath character. There was no question but that the Giants were the Davids, and there was no question of which was the right side to be on, especially since the home-towners were getting beat up so badly. Fans could come out and joyfully cheer on the Giants and not be disappointed when they lost. More people, relaxed, came to the games to cheer (and laugh at) the underdog. It was nice to be seen there, like conspicuous consuming. Girls went alone or in pairs, and so did boys. Candlestick Park became a good place to meet other people, and maybe go home with them. It was an even better place to go once the management added white wine (served in little plastic goblets) and a remarkable mini-quiche to its choice of food. Still more people came.

At first, the players resented being laughed at, but soon they joined in the good humor of it all and actually played better, losing less frequently. Attendance jumped again when civil service employees from around the Bay Area made the Giants their favorites and came from as far as Milpitas. Civil servants from other major-league cities got the message. When the Giants were on the road they began to find themselves cheered on by whole sections of fans. These were local municipal employees coming to support the visitors. Hell, they were civil service brothers all. It was possible to identify with the Giants, and they needed a helping hand. So the city employees of St. Louis came to cheer the Giants and boo the Cards. The Cards muttered about the fickle nature of their fans and went into a slump, losing four straight to the Giants.

Team morale rose, then skyrocketed when, in New York, some civil service groupies showed up to give the boys their support. Jocks were jocks, after all, regardless of their civil status. The Giants took two of three from the Mets, and then murdered the Expos in three straight after someone translated the French banners, "*L'union fait la force – Vive les Giants.*" Some young kids out in Walnut Creek were bugging their parents to move to San Francisco so they might have a chance to make the Giants' civil service-regulated team. This was not lost on city politicians and city planners, who for years had been looking for ways to stop the flight of middle-class families to the suburbs. Local baseball might just succeed where lousy schools had failed.

By the time the Giants returned from their road trip toward the end of July, they were a relaxed, winning bunch of guys. Morale was at an all-time high, and they were playing over their heads: a 10- or 20-game fluke, perhaps, but fun nevertheless. As attendances rose, the team continued to play well. However, despite the improvement, they were still 14 games out of first place at the end of the month, and everyone assumed that they were too far behind ever to catch up.

Then, in early August, two stars of the hated, league-leading Dodgers announced that they were playing out their options and would toil for whichever teams would pay them the most millions the next year. The two were each pocketing about a million dollars a year. That made the Giants, with their civil service aura, even more popular. (Management wasn't talking about how much three or four of *their* stars were making, or that 15 of the Giants were planning to do exactly the same thing as the two ungrateful Dodgers.) The Dodgers went into a slump with the announcement of the impending defections and dropped nine straight, four of them to the Giants on a memorable weekend when 250,000 people squeezed through Candlestick's turnstiles to see the civil service home team.

By the end of August, the Giants were only four games out of first place and were driving hard. At that point, Fidel Castro announced that he would love to come to the World Series if the Giants were in it. The idea of a public, socialist team was inspiring and could only help Cuban–U.S. relations. Even people from Haight–Ashbury started coming to games after Fidel's announcement. The Giants took over first place on September 15, won another three straight in Atlanta, and led the pack by three games on the 20th.

San Francisco was a madhouse. There were only two weeks left in the season. Orders for World Series tickets started pouring in. Every hotel room was booked in anticipation. The papers and television were full of the Giants. No team had ever come from 25 games behind to win a pennant. And this was a civil service team! Howard Cosell marveled over "the incredible vitality of *this* team and *this* town, the *City* by the *Golden Gate.*"

In city hall, more than one observer commented that the workers there seemed to be standing straighter and taller than usual. They were also dressing better (fewer combinations of jackets and pants from different suits of slightly different colors) and seemed to have a shine about them. The level of public service hadn't changed, but it was a more purposeful inefficiency. The Mayor recalled that he had predicted a new era, and Governor Brown reminded everyone that the idea had been his in the first place. Hadrian Ness was being wooed by the city attorney to take an important, high-paying job, but was holding out for tenured status. Manager Grubb was getting a divorce, but that didn't bother him since he was becoming a celebrity. He also had a wonderful, built-in scapegoat for the few occasions when the Giants lost. He could publicly berate the performance of his third-base coach: "How can I manage when the civil service makes me keep people like that?" No one could blame him if they failed every so often. He had no control over the dolts. The team's success under such circumstances was due to his superior managing, the wonderful San Francisco fans, and a solid core of dedicated players.

On September 21, late in a game with Chicago that the Giants were leading by eight runs, the third-base coach had Bill Murphy, one of the dedicated ones, try to steal home for what would have been a superfluous score. Kretch, the Chicago pitcher, furious that the Giants were adding insult to injury, threw his best pitch of the game directly at Murphy. The ball broke Murphy's leg. Murphy, the second baseman, was a steady but not outstanding member of the team. He just did his job, and a lot of people didn't even know his name, so it didn't seem to be a crucial loss, at least not until the new second baseman showed up the next day.

Gussie Johnson, sent by the civil service to replace Murphy, was a big, strapping, fast, San Francisco-bred Chinese slugger who had been batting .420 in the minors (albeit with the Golden Gate Park Dunes). The only trouble with Gussie was that he was left-handed. Manager Grubb was livid. He screamed to D'Orsi that it was impossible to have a left-handed second baseman: a southpaw couldn't make the necessary pivot on double plays. There had never been a left-handed second baseman in the history of baseball. Just ask Cosell. D'Orsi, as ever, was calm amid the onslaught. She pointed out that Grubb was just using an old, old ploy of all the other department heads to undermine the civil service merit system: they were always trying to create so-called "specialist" positions, geared to particular people, rather than general positions where many applicants could compete and get jobs by merit. Only recently, the city's planning director had been caught trying to create something called an "urban designer" position, when it was clear that a city planner was always a city planner. Just because the planner who passed first had a background in political economics (Marxism), there was no reason to think he couldn't design a park as well as the next planner. An infielder was an infielder, by God, and let's hear no more of this specialist second baseman subcategory nonsense. Besides, Gussie had competed in a well-advertised exam and had come out on top. It made no difference to D'Orsi that he had got such a high score partly by virtue of the extra points that came his way automatically as an armed forces veteran.

D'Orsi also told Grubb that she had observed that there were no Chinese players on the ball team. Was Grubb living testimony that the bureaucracy was bigoted? Was he looking for a civil rights suit? D'Orsi told Grubb that the civil service union watched her every step. She was powerless; she couldn't set a precedent for the rest of the civil service. The union's attorneys would have the matter in the courts for months, and in the meantime Grubb would have no second baseman, not even a left-handed one. Anyway, if Gussie didn't work out, then Grubb had the right to terminate him during the first six months, if he could come up with a good reason. Grubb perked up at this, but only until he realized that two of the next three people on the "infielder" list were over 45 (but under 60), part of a new "Not So Senior" minority group that was emerging in San

Francisco. The third was known to be active in the women's movement. The fourth in line might be a winner – he was young and didn't know anything except how to play baseball – but he was much too far down the list to offer Grubb any real hope.

Grubb wandered unsteadily back to Candlestick Park. That afternoon Gussie had four hits and scored two runs. In the ninth inning, score tied 2–2, bases loaded, one out, the Cubs' batter hit solidly to the Giants' shortstop, who threw to second base for one out. But Johnson's slow relay to first was not in time to catch the batter for a double play. A run, the winning run, was duly scored from third. D'Orsi listened to the game in her office at city hall and was ecstatic about Gussie's hitting. The Giants were still two games ahead, and the next day Grubb moved his right-handed third baseman to second and tried Gussie at third.

By then, Two-Fingered Brown, a back-up catcher that the civil service had sent, was on the team. Brown had a rifle arm but no control of where the ball went when he threw it. That characteristic hadn't been spotted in the civil service exam, which was three-quarters written (testing the player's knowledge of baseball) and just one-quarter playing in the field. Brown, a big reader, had done magnificently on the written exam (100 percent), so it didn't matter that he scored only 40 on the playing part. His combined score of 85 was more than enough to pass, and the 15 extra points he got for being handicapped meant he came out on top of all the applicants.

Brown had a mania for trying to pick off runners at first base, having done so once successfully in the little league ten years earlier, when he had his full complement of fingers. In a game against Houston, two days after the Gussie Johnson incident, Brown tried to pick off yet another runner at first. The throw, like a shot, hit pitcher Montefusco on the kneecap, and that was all for Montefusco for the season and for the Giants that day.

It wasn't all for Two-Fingered Brown, though. Immediately after the game, Grubb fired him, and the dismissal was upheld. (Brown was still in his probationary period, when department heads had absolute discretionary rights.) However, as a gesture of kindness and humanity (Brown had two wives and three kids to support), the Civil Service Commission directed that his name must be returned to the bottom of the civil service "catchers list," so that he might have a chance with some other department. D'Orsi didn't point out to the commissioners that no other city department used catchers, two-fingered ones least of all. As luck would have it, no one else was on the catchers list at that time (the others who had passed the exam had since left town), so the bottom of the list was also the top. Consequently, Brown was back with the Giants, duly certified, the next day.

The Giants' lead was down to one game. The season was drawing to a close.

There are people in San Francisco who will tell you that the 1980 season ended the next day, when a new outfielder showed up – in a wheelchair. Most people know that never really happened; it was a prank pulled by the visiting

Dodgers. However, Grubb did have a nervous breakdown the next day. Whether it was due to the Two-Fingered Brown incident, or the Gussie Johnson affair, or the third-base coach's affair with his wife, or his hatred of D'Orsi, or one of a thousand other reasons is hard to say. Civil service psychologists at San Francisco General Hospital still search, over coffee breaks, for a credible answer.

Some will tell you that San Franciscans live in their own world. They will tell you that there *was* a World Series in 1980, as in other years, and that to hear people talk around city hall, the civil service Giants were in it – or could have been.

For some people in San Francisco, it is still September. October and the World Series are just around the corner, and the Giants might damned well make it. All they need is a good, left-handed first baseman, and there's a terrific prospect just waiting to win it all for the Giants. He was second on the civil service list. The new manager, an expert from Berkeley's School of Public Policy (they are experts in everything, including baseball management), is in the process of firing the right-handed top-of-the-list first baseman that the civil service sent, but that could take a while because the case is being appealed.

Some city hall watchers will tell you it is Monday of the last week of the regular season, and that the Civil Service Commission will be meeting this very afternoon to decide the issue. It's on their agenda. They will tell you that there is great expectation in the Giants' offices and dressing rooms in Candlestick Park. The Giants are only one game behind and a pennant is still in sight.

A civil service clerk, on the staff of the Civil Service Commission, will tell you, just as he told his wife five minutes ago during his break, that a lawyer for the civil service union, representing the right-handed first baseman, has requested a postponement, and that such requests are almost always granted. Maybe they will decide the matter next week. Maybe the season won't end.

Part IX

The Good City

San Francisco, Noe Valley, day

Most people live in cities, and more will. People living in close proximity to one another, in a given area, is one of the definitions of city or urban. Of course, if you use one of the United States Census criteria for urban, 1,000 people living in a square mile, you get about three people or one house per acre, assuming that half of the square mile is for housing. I would hardly call that urban or city. That's closer to being a farm than a city, I think. I live in San Francisco, and many people consider it to be a fine city, particularly people from Europe, who rate it with New York and Boston as America's best. Americans seem to like it, too, particularly if one judges by all of those who seem to want to live there, making housing prices insanely high, impossible for the likes of school teachers, government employees, sales and service workers, blue-collar workers (there still are some), and just plain folks to afford. But there is a lot of "goodness" in San Francisco hills and trees, the water, lots of small properties with modest-scaled buildings, a good climate, reasonably clear air, a fair transit system, a diverse population, great eating, a public that participates in its governance, Golden Gate Park and the Presidio, an easily accessible, productive, and beautiful hinterland, lots of cultural stuff, and more. At the same time, the public rights-of-way, for the most part, leave a lot to be desired. And, of late, the last 10 to 15 years, we have seen huge, out-of-scale development that has paid no attention to adopted city plans. Bad new things can outweigh good new things, like the new ball park and the Academy of Science.

Vancouver, on the other hand, is getting better: the best public waterfront in the world and always expanding, it seems, an understanding of what makes good, enjoyable, walkable streets and neighborhoods, wonderful and accessible parks, great street trees, easy to get around, by foot, bicycle, transit or auto, a quiet gentleness, views, good shopping streets with lots of local merchants, an easy place to live.

Maybe I'm too close to San Francisco and see its problems more easily than I see Vancouver's, or those of Portland, a small big city that seems very concerned with publicness, building well in very small city blocks, making public transit really work, and environmental responsibility. I have real problems with places like Phoenix, which I cannot bring myself to think of as a city; it's more of a developed area. The waste of land with low-density, sprawling development borders on the criminal, all the more so because of the waste of that most precious of commodities, water, and the air pollution generated by the auto culture. It's hard to believe that people with tuberculosis once moved there for the clean air.

Kansas City and Cleveland represent another city type: cities that once were. The vast areas of vacant or empty once-urban land leave one breathless, and depressed. Knowing how they came to be what they are doesn't help. Reforestation and "urban" agriculture would be among the wonderful, productive futures for places like that, but those alternatives don't seem to interest people.

Experiencing those cities, and many more, over much of the world – not all, for sure – leads me to a question or two or three. What is or would be a good city? What are the qualities of a good city to be achieved, striven for? How would we build cities that would achieve those qualities, or at least be more likely to achieve them than would be other ways of building?

In a good city, the air would be clean. Normally, in a day's comings and goings, one wouldn't even think about the air. The same should be said about most of the important parts of city life; the qualities of a good city. For sure, there would be opportunities to learn and to work, to earn one's livelihood; and places to get to, with ease, places for social interaction or just to see other people, or places to be alone; and opportunities to participate in local decisions; and places for fun. If, in our daily lives, we, collectively, put little or nothing into the air that might dirty it, then presumably we would have achieved clean air; or, better yet, the already clean air would stay that way. So, we shouldn't put dirty things in the air. Multiple places to work, nearby, would offer a variety of employment possibilities. Finding a variety of locations for employment, many close to where people live, shouldn't be all that difficult. And public places for people to meet, sit, talk, or be alone and in "natural" settings respond to needs for social interaction and inner contemplation. That's what plazas, parks, and natural landscapes are all about.

Some physical qualities are more likely than others to achieve our environmental, social, and economic objectives. When we have city building choices to make, and there are many, from little ones like trees along a street or how to pave a sidewalk, to big ones like how to lay out a new city or expand one that exists, we should choose the ones most likely to be consonant with or achieve good city objectives. My close colleague Donald Appleyard and I, some years ago, wrote what we then called "Toward an Urban Design Manifesto." We were concerned with the qualities of people's everyday lives and how the physical design of cities might help achieve good cities. We started with what we called essential "goals," the first of which was *livability*. Livability starts with the most basic things: clean air, clean water, a well-managed environment relatively devoid of dirt, trash, noise, danger, overcrowding; a physically healthy living environment. It means, as well, places where people can live in relative comfort. Most people want a sanctuary for their immediate living environment, a place where they can bring up children, enjoy privacy, sleep, eat, relax, and restore themselves. Like the other goals, this one, and all the aspects of it, of urban, city livability, would be for everyone, in well-to-do and developing cities alike.

Cities should provide and people should have access to *opportunity, imagination, and joy*. On the basic livelihood side, people should have access to work choices, and the closer to home the better. And they should have access to affordable alternative housing possibilities. At the same time, the good city would offer places where people can break from traditional molds, extend their experience, meet new people, learn other viewpoints. A city should have magical places where fantasy is possible, counters to and escapes from the mundanity of everyday work and living. Good cities have always been places of excitement; theaters, with stages upon which citizens can display themselves and see others; public spaces, signs, lights, movement, color. There can be parts of the city where belief can be suspended. One should not have to travel as far as the Himalayas or the South Sea islands or Disneyland or Las Vegas to stretch one's experience. Such challenges could be nearer home, for community utopias, for historic, natural, and anthropological evocations of the modern city, for encounters with the truly exotic. For sure, much imagination and much joy are embedded within individuals, but the good city can encourage their development and afford them the license they need.

People should be able to understand the form and basic layout of their city as well as its environmental context and the interrelationships between the two. This means an understanding of the climate, the land, the water in and around the city, and the opportunities and constraints that these afford for daily life. Urban *authenticity and meaning* include knowing and valuing where food comes from, what grows where one lives, and what does not. An authentic city is one where the origins of things and places are clear. The city form as well as its institutions should help to educate its citizens about the natural setting as well as an understanding of why things are where they are, and something of their histories. The recreated wetlands at Crissy Field, in San Francisco's Presidio, tell people what that whole northern shoreline was once like at the same time as the old airplane hangars reveal that all that land was once filled in to create a military airport. A leftover railroad crossing sign in a park at the upscale Golden Gateway housing development suggested an earlier blue-collar history. Sadly, it was removed: what harm was it doing anyone? A city should present itself as a readable story, in an engaging and, if necessary, provocative way; for people are indifferent to the obvious, overwhelmed by complexity. A city's offerings should be revealed or they will be missed.

People should feel that some part of the urban environment belongs to them, individually and collectively, some part for which they care and are responsible, irrespective of whether they own it. The city environment should be one that encourages participation. Some urbanites may not always want this, preferring anonymity. But I am not convinced that anonymity should be designed for. It would be much better if people were sure enough of themselves to stand up and be counted. Environments should be designed for people who use them or are affected by them (and in this sense I do not include corporations, who are anonymous people). City design should increase people's sense of identity and rootedness and encourage care and responsibility for the physical environment. *Conservation* encourages identity, control, and, usually, a better sense of community, since older environments are more a part of common heritage.

Livability, opportunity, identity, and authenticity are qualities of the good city that should serve the individual and small social unit, but the city has to serve some higher social goals as well. A city should breed a commitment to tolerance, justice, law, and democracy, and to the wholeness of community, not only to neighborhoods. The physical structure of the city should invite and encourage *community and public life*, not only through institutions but directly and symbolically through public spaces. The public environment, by definition, should be open to all members of the community. It is where people of different kinds meet. No one should be excluded unless they threaten the balance of that life.

Cities should strive to be *self-sustaining*. This is particularly true in regard to the use and reuse of natural resources and the disposal of waste. Amazing amounts of needed food and fiber can and should be grown within cities or immediately adjacent to them, within a one night's journey. Street trees can produce crops, parks can have orchards and still be parks, the variations of possible community or private food-growing gardens are endless and large; productive fields in and adjacent to built-up areas have long histories. Scarce resources, especially water and increasingly air, should be carefully husbanded, not wasted. "Soft energy paths," wind, water, farm products, rather than exploitation across regions and countries, will help establish a strong sense of regional identity, authenticity, and meaning for the good city. Seeing and being familiar with what happens to our wastes, human and mechanical, and being individually responsible for at least some of its disposal would breed care in what and how much we consume. The locations of cities would be much more carefully considered and very differently laid out than is now the case if urban self-reliance were an important objective. What would Phoenix and Las Vegas be like? Certainly not like what they are.

Good cities should be *accessible to all*. Every citizen is entitled to environmental livability and levels of identity, control, and opportunity. Good cities and good urban design must be for the less well-to-do as well as for the rich. Indeed, they are *more* needed by the poor. The good city is pluralistic, where power is reasonably distributed among social groups, but where different values and cultures of interest- and place-based groups are acknowledged and negotiated in a just public arena. Governing, formally and informally, should be accessible, too. As a modest, simple example, the physical accessibility of San Francisco's city hall is impressive – not much more than a half-hour trip by public transit from any part of the city. And the building's grandness helps; the people's visual focal point.

Achieving the good city is a complex matter, of course. The things that we seek and strive for are often in conflict with each other. The more a city promises for the individual, the less it seems to have a public life; the more the city is built for public entities, the less the individual seems to count. Balance is rarely easy but the good city is one that somehow balances these goals, allowing individual and group identity while maintaining a public concern, encouraging pleasure while maintaining responsibility, remaining open to outsiders while sustaining a strong sense of localism, using the natural environment while at the same time conserving it.

It is possible to arrange cities and metropolitan regions, physically, in ways that are more likely to achieve the environmental, social, and economic qualities we seek than are other arrangements. Thousands and thousands of communal as well as private decisions, at large and minute scales, are regularly made that impact the future city, good or bad. A street tree can give shade, a wide turning radius at a corner will encourage drivers to go around it quickly, a large shopping mall at the outskirts of town may be convenient for new suburban families, but might drain the older town center of businesses and people. Take a look at central Kansas City at the start of the 21st century.

What, then, would be a buildable urban fabric for an urban life, the good city? People, as I have said, should be able to live in reasonable safety, cleanliness, and security. That means *livable streets and neighborhoods*, with adequate sunlight, clean air, trees, vegetation, gardens, open space, pleasantly scaled and designed buildings. Most streets would be lined with buildings with minimal or no setbacks and little space between them, creating a street wall. Driveways, for cars, would be minimal, if present at all. More often than not, vehicle parking spaces for individual homes would be off alleyways. Deciduous trees, rarely more than one species to a block, would give shade in the summer, allow sun in winter. Where trees are not appropriate, or are alien to the land and climate (San Francisco may be such a place), the buildings themselves would be oriented to create shadow or allow sunlight. Streets and the buildings along them would, in short, encourage people to walk. Most streets, then, would be designed for a pedestrian pace, including the shopping streets. Private vehicles might well be accommodated, but not overly catered to. Nor would large private vehicles be the determinants of street sizes. Public safety, fire and police, and refuse disposal would be achieved with sensibly modest-scaled vehicles. Paving would allow water filtration and self-cleaning.

In the good city, there would be streets for concentrations of people as well as for goods movement over medium and long distances. Those streets would be within easy walking distances of where people live and work because the major public transit lines – streetcars, buses, rapid transit – would be concentrated on them, and so might be faster-moving private vehicles. But most of these streets, too, would serve many types of movement, not only one or two. Pedestrians and bicycles would be welcomed. These streets would have to be wider than others and, as such, would stand out. It is quite possible that they would be major determinants of a remembered physical structure of the city – the "Main" street, the "High" street, the "Center" street. Large commercial uses and points of focus might well locate on some of them. Some special-purpose streets would be necessary, for trucks in heavy industrial areas, for example, but these would be few.

The layout of streets, public ways, is fundamentally a public function and this would be understood in the good city. Of the man-made impositions on the land, streets, more than anything else, determine the form and function and ultimately the character of cities. There would be many intersections of streets so that people, however they travel, have lots of choices of how to proceed, how to get where they want to go. Small blocks are more likely to offer a human, walkable scale than are large ones. If someone or some company or institution needed or was fortunate enough to have a whole block, the likelihood of large-scale, cordoned-off, internally oriented rather than street-oriented development would be less than is the case with large blocks.

The so-called "business district" of Irvine, California, may be the foremost example of everything that is bad about large-block development. In the 1990s, a remarkably progressive mayor of Irvine, Larry Agran, was concerned that his city had no downtown, had few people walking, and had a lot of air pollution. (The absence of downtown and lack of walking were pointed out to Agran by his mother, who was visiting from the East.) Shown very simple maps of San Francisco, Portland, Santa Monica, even parts of Los Angeles, as well as of his own city, his mouth dropped and he said, "That explains it!" San Francisco has about 216 blocks and 293 intersections in one square mile of its downtown. Irvine has just 17 blocks and 15 intersections. Portland, on the other hand, has 318 small blocks, 200 feet on a side, and 370 intersections in a square mile. In Portland, there can be many buildings and lots, 16 if the parcels are 25 feet wide and 100 feet deep, or few, one to four in many downtown blocks. But in either case, the scale is relatively small and there are usually many entrances along the streets. Even when there is only one building and one entrance, it's not very far to another public street. Given that street and block pattern and a strong, lasting predisposition against abandoning public rights-of-way, the big space users have somehow managed to build on the modest parcels; even supermarkets, which provide lots of parking underneath. Look at a simple map of Portland, downtown or uptown, and it is nothing special to behold. But *visit* Portland, experience its scale, the welcoming nature of its streets, the ability to choose, at each of the many intersections, where you want to go next, and you soon realize that this is a good city.

A good city is likely to have many parcels of land and many buildings, rather than just a few. With many small parcels and buildings, there is much more likelihood of many caretakers of properties and consequently more people with a sense of ownership, responsibility, control, and felt interest in participation in the community. Sure, the tendency to large, singly designed and developed parcels with few buildings and many joint owners – condominiums – seems to be the economic way of development in the new millennium. But even when these developments are done well, with many seemingly separate housing or commercial units, the participation in them, the direct responsibility for maintenance, and even the opportunity to paint one's unit an unpopular color are less than with many distinct parcels and buildings. For a long time we have been led to believe that large landholdings are necessary to design healthy, efficient, aesthetically pleasing urban environments. The slums of the industrial city were associated with all those small, overbuilt parcels. Socialist and capitalist ideologies alike called for land assembly to permit integrated, socially and economically useful developments. What the socialist countries did via public ownership, the capitalists did through redevelopment and new fiscal mechanisms that rewarded large holdings. Architects of both ideological persuasions promulgated or were easily convinced of the wisdom of land assembly. The results, whether by big business or by big government, or the two combined, are more often than not inward-oriented, easily controlled or controllable large building projects with fewer entrances, fewer windows, less diversity, less innovation, and less individual expression than an urban fabric that can be achieved with many actors and many buildings, a result that is more likely to grow out of many parcels. Just as reasonable public controls can avoid the health-and-safety issues attendant on overdevelopment of small parcels, so they can be directed to larger parcels to achieve many of the physical qualities we seek. The North False Creek and downtown areas of Vancouver are excellent examples. But socio-economic qualities of ownership, a personal stake, having a piece of the public action, and participation are more likely with many parcels and buildings. With smaller buildings and parcels, more entrances must be located on public spaces; consequently, more windows and a finer scale of design diversity emerge. A more public, lively city is produced.

Of course, there is a need for larger buildings, too, covering large areas of land, but they will be the exceptions in the good city, not the rule. Public buildings, city hall, the main library, the public courts building, museums, and churches may all qualify; corporate or private offices should not.

Cities are not farms. A city is people living and working and doing the things they do in relatively close proximity to each other. So a *minimum density* is needed in the good city. To be sure, to a considerable degree, density – the number of people living on an area of land or the number of people using an area of land – is in part a perceived phenomenon and therefore relative to the beholder. For many purposes, perceived density is more important than an "objective" measurement of people per unit of land. Though physical phenomena can be manipulated so as to render perceptions of greater or lesser density, some minimum number of people living and using a given area is required if there is to be human exchange, public life and action, diversity, and community.

Density of people alone will account for the presence or absence of certain uses and services important to urban life. The number and diversity of small stores and services – groceries, bars, bakeries, cleaners and laundries, coffee shops, second-hand stores – to be found in a city, within hailing distance of where one lives, is in part a function of density. Such businesses are more likely to exist, and be present in greater variety, in an area where people live in greater proximity to each other. The viability of mass transit depends partly on the density of residential areas and partly on the size and intensity of activity at commercial and service destinations. More use of transit reduces auto-parking demands and permits increases in density. The goal of local control and community identity is associated with density as well. The notion of an optimum density is elusive and is easily confused with the health and livability of urban areas, with lifestyles, with housing types, and with the economics of development. Energy efficiency is also a concern associated with density; conservation of land and fuel demanding more compact living arrangements.

A minimum net density (people or living units divided by the size of the building site, excluding public streets) of about 15 dwelling units (or 30 to 60 people) per acre of land is necessary to support city life. Generous town houses or row houses on parcels up to 25 feet wide and 100 feet deep would produce such densities, but so would other building types, with ease. You don't get cities at six dwellings to the acre, let alone on half-acre lots. On the other hand, it is possible to go as high as 48 dwelling units per acre (96 to 192 people) and still provide for a spacious, gracious urban life. Much of San Francisco was developed with three-storey buildings (one large unit per floor above a parking storey) on parcels 25 feet by 100 (or 125) feet. At those densities, with that kind of housing, there can be private or shared gardens for most people, no common hallways are required, and people can have direct access to the ground. Public streets and walks adequate to handle pedestrian, bicycle, and vehicular traffic generated by these densities can be accommodated in rights-of-way that are 50 feet wide, or less. Higher densities, for parts of the city, to suit particular needs and lifestyles, would be possible and desirable. Upper density limits? That's a tough question but the suspicion is that as the numbers get much higher than 250 people per net residential acre for large parts of the city, the concessions to less desirable living arrangements begin to mount.

Beyond residential density, there must be a minimum intensity of people using an area for it to be urban. Here, too, numbers are illusive. Public meeting areas require people who can get to them with ease, walking or cycling for the most part; city or neighborhood focal points or lineal paths with shops and public services. The lowest residential densities, the 15 dwelling units per acre, will provide most meeting areas with life and human exchange, but may not generate enough activity for the most intense central districts. In the good city, there is an *integration of activities*: living, working, and shopping as well as public, spiritual, and recreational activities reasonably near each other.

Good urban places have some mixtures of usage, responding to the values of publicness and diversity that encourage local community identity – excitement, spirit, sense stimulation, and exchange are more likely when there is a mixture of activities than when there is not. It is the mix, not just the density of people, that brings life to an area, the life of people going about a full range of normal activities without having to get into an automobile.

It would probably not be possible for every area of the city to have a full mix of uses. There is a lot to be said for "living sanctuaries," which consist almost wholly of housing. But such areas should not dominate the city, should be relatively small, of a few blocks, and should be close and easily accessible, by foot, to areas where people meet to shop or work or recreate, or grow things or do public business. And, except for a few of the most intensely developed office blocks of a business district or a heavy industrial area, the meeting areas should have housing within them. Stores should be mixed with offices. Envisioning the urban landscape as a cloth, it would be a salt-and-pepper fabric of many colors, with each color for a separate use or a combination of uses. Some areas would be much more heavily one color than another; some would be an even mix of colors. Some areas, if you squinted or got so close that you saw only a small part of the fabric, would read as one color. But by and large there might be few distinct patterns except for those created by an open-space system or by the understandable network of public ways that gives the city its distinct form.

Buildings and other objects placed in the environment are arranged in such ways as to define and even enclose public space, rather than sit in space. It is not enough to have high densities and an integration of activities to have a good city. Buildings close to each other, along a street, regardless of whether the street is straight, curved, or angled, tend to define space if the street is not too wide in relation to the buildings. The same holds for a plaza or a square. As the spaces between buildings become larger, the buildings tend more and more to sit in space. They become things to look at for few or many people. That's fine for the Washington Monument or the Lincoln Memorial, or a sports stadium, but otherwise buildings in space tend to be private and inward oriented. Avoiding a temptation to ascribe all kinds of psychological values to defined spaces, such as intimacy, belonging, protection, which are difficult to prove; it is enough to observe that spaces surrounded by buildings are more likely to bring people together and thereby promote public interaction. Interest and interplay among uses are enhanced. To be sure, such arrangements direct people and limit their freedom – they cannot move in any direction from any point – but presumably there are enough choices left open to them, and the gain is in the greater potential for sense stimulation, excitement, surprise, and focus. We seek out and return to defined ways and spaces as symbolic of urban life, emphasizing the public space more than the private building.

The good city emphasizes and celebrates *public places and a public way system*. The central value of urban life is publicness: of people of different groups meeting each other and of people acting in concert, albeit with debate; of people achieving together what they cannot achieve alone. The most important public places are for pedestrians, for no public life can take place between people in automobiles. People of different kinds meet each other directly in public places. The level of communication may be only visual, but that in itself is educational and can encourage tolerance. Street activities, street vending, and street theater can be the precursors of a more flourishing public environment. There are also public meeting places, accessible to all and publicly controlled.

Public places include parks, playgrounds, and community centers within easy walking distances of where people live, to provide access to nature, relief from the built environment, locations for active recreation, and the like. Where cities meet water – shorelines along rivers, lakes, bays, oceans – there will be linear parks and promenades, as well as beaches for healthy, joyful living. Often these will be the locations of special, environmentally fragile and important sites, wetlands, bird and animal habitats, visible to people, but held sacred. Often, highest points will also be kept open.

In order to communicate, to get from place to place, to interact, to exchange ideas and goods, the good city will have a healthy, public circulation system. It cannot be privately controlled. Public circulation systems are seen as significant cultural settings where the city's finest products and artifacts can be displayed. Circulation within the city has an easily understood set of priorities, determined largely by the detailed designs of streets and other public ways: pedestrians, public transit, bicycles, private automobiles, delivery vehicles. A key to design, here, is an understanding that on many streets, maybe most, all of these uses can exist together, but at a pedestrian pace. There is a need for emergency vehicles as well, police and fire, but these need not be oversized behemoths. Of course, there is also a need for some streets where rather fast-paced vehicular traffic can pass – traffic going through or around the city, or to and from it from different points – or for heavy and bulky goods. But these will be the exceptions, and even they will be pleasant places to be and will often accommodate other movement needs as well.

Depending on the size of the good city, there will be one or more major centers of activity: commerce, offices, buying and selling, services, government, recognized areas of community focus. In many ways they will be different than the more modest living–working areas only in their intensity of uses and because they will be major destination areas for citywide public transit. They will still have living areas within them, so they will always be peopled. If the city is large enough, there may be major centers for special purposes, such as a civic center. Boundaries – physical features that define limits, locations, and identity to make neighborhoods, and the city itself – will be common, but sometimes vague.

As an urban fabric, the physical, designable qualities stand a fine chance of meeting many of the goals of what a good city should be. They directly attend to the issue of livability though they are aimed especially at encouraging public spaces and public life. They attend to environmental responsibility. Their efforts in personal and group identity are less clear, though the small-scale city is more likely than the large-scale city to support identity. Opportunity and imagination should be encouraged by a diverse and densely settled urban structure. This structure should also create a setting that is more meaningful than giant environments to the individual inhabitants and small groups. There is no guarantee that this urban environment will be more just than those presently in existence. In supporting the small against the large, however, more justice for the powerless may be encouraged. And balance is critical. Density without livability could return us to the slums of the 19th century. Public places without small-scale, fine-grain development would give us vast, overscaled cities.

While the concentration here is on defining physical characteristics of a good city fabric, the process of creating it is crucial. As important as many buildings and spaces are the *many participants* in the city-building process. It is through this involvement in the creation and management of their city that citizens will be most likely to identify with it and, conversely, enhance their own sense of identity and control.

San Francisco, Noe Valley, night

Index